The Journey

An Uplifting True Story of An Immigrant Escaping Repression in Iran, Building the American Dream in Colorado, and Seeking Peace of Mind and Heart in New Zealand

Twin Lakes Publishing, Inc.
www.twinlakespublishing.com

Firooz Eftekhar Zadeh

To Mary Clark With Best Wishes Firooz Zadeh 29/2/2013

ISBN 0-9674480-2-6

Library of Congress Control Number: 2003113502

Printed January 2004
www.twinlakespublishing.com

Cover by: Pearson Design, Evergreen, CO.

An Immigrant's Story

Some people changed countries because
the land seemed more fertile on the other
side of the ocean; others were wrenched
away. Some sought a livelihood; others
sought protection. Some came a hundred
years ago; others came only yesterday.
Some were afraid of political change;
others had to run for lives.

People say it takes five years for an
uprooted tree to take root again and
begin growing in the new soil. But,
how long does it take for a person?

CONTENTS

Acknowledgments

I owe a special thank you to Cheryl Fluehr, the wonderful entertainment manager of the Holland America Cruise Lines for giving me the opportunity to present my lectures to their intelligent and outstanding passengers who encouraged me to write this book.

I am indebted to Mike Bullock for his skillful editing of the first edition, <u>From Tehran to Twin Lakes.</u>

I am very fortunate to have a great friend, Dr. Albert Dawson an invaluable editor for his patience and knowledge in correcting my English.

My greatest praise goes to my lovely wife, Bernadette. She gives me her love, and a life I only dreamt about. I could not have published this book without her valuable support and unflinching help.

The love for my two daughters has always been a constant inspiration in my life that provides me an enormous energy for wanting to do more and accomplish the seemingly impossible.

All the names used in this story are fictitious in an effort to protect the privacy and security of all persons involved.

Dedication

This book is dedicated first and foremost to Tala, the most influential person in my life, my paternal grandmother, an exceptional human being who taught me to reach for the highest possible goal.

She gave me hope, inspiration, and determination which I needed to survive under the toughest living conditions. It was her effective teaching that made me who I am today.

Also this is dedicated to my precious sister, Ziba, who at the age of thirteen became my personal nurse and saved my life.

I am indebted to all my friends and family in Iran who encouraged me to pursue an athletic career and later assisted me in escaping Iran for a better life in America. I also owe my happy life to my American friends, especially the gracious people in Laramie, Wyoming, and the Colorado communities. I would like to express my gratitude to the many wonderful people, who supported and befriended me along the way by making me feel welcome, successful, and part of their families in the United States.

Last but not least, to all my friends in Nelson, New Zealand who helped me with their special warmth and exuberant personalities to make a home in their beautiful country where I expect to live in peace in the remaining happy years of my life.

My true dedicatory thanks are to you, the reader, for taking the time to peruse this story about the human spirit's struggle for survival.

It has not been easy to relive and relate all the painful details of this life; however, if I can encourage and put hope in one person's heart, I feel that I have fulfilled my passion of sharing the heartache and the resultant successes.

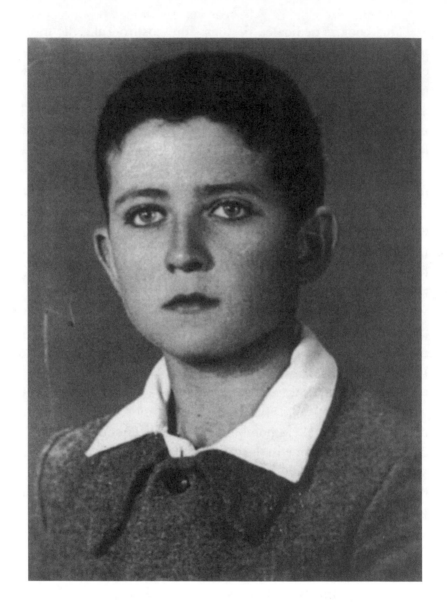

Preface

I believe that whatever the reasons are for leaving one's own country, it can be a positive move, providing one is aware, realistic, and cognizant of the challenges to be faced. It is my desire to assist the reader in understanding how difficult life in Iran is and problems that the Middle East immigrants have in adjusting to their new lives and culture in other countries.

This story is told from the heart and its purpose is threefold. First, I wish to share my life as an immigrant and, hopefully, to inspire other immigrants in their quest for a brighter future. Second, I want to help people to understand the difficulties Middle Eastern immigrants face in establishing roots in new countries. Third, I hope to inspire readers by sharing a true survival and success story which proves that with determination the human spirit can overcome adverse circumstances.

Traveling throughout the United States, Canada, Europe, Asia, the Middle East, South America, Australia, and New Zealand during the past fifteen years has given me the opportunity to converse with many immigrants. The feedback I have received has shown that the problems are universal. Language, specifically slang, customs, religion, morals, family conflicts, cultural differences often are serious barriers in understanding, conforming, and assimilating to a new life. I admire all those who persevered, beat the odds, and succeeded in their dreams.

Born into a wealthy Iranian family in 1938, I ironically was denied food, clothing, and affection because I had an abusive father, an uncaring mother, and a mean stepmother. My youthful life was one of constant struggle. Deprivation, starvation, and physical abuse are my unhappy childhood memories. Survival for the children of the Middle East with powerty, corruption, over population, lack of education, wars, and many unpleasant conditions has become quite difficult. These harsh conditions made me learn at an early age to rely on myself and my own resources.

I could easily have grown up to be the typical poor Iranian boy selling postcards or shining shoes in the streets, destined for a career as a vendor of sunglasses. Instead, as a child I imagined myself a star soccer player in a big stadium. In my dreams, I was able to transform the mad honking of horns in our daily dangerous traffic congestion into cheering fans and athletic triumphs. My fantasies became a reality at the age of nineteen when I became a member of the Iranian national soccer team. By 1960, I dreamed of coming to the United States. It took seven long, arduous years to compile, complete, and remit numerous mandatory admission forms to enter my new country with a student visa.

I immigrated in 1967 with my wife, daughter, and three suitcases. In lieu of money, I had an education, motivation, ambition, integrity, and a dream. Leaving my motherland gave me the freedom to pursue and explore career opportunities in a democratic society.

I thought my trials and tribulations were over when I came to America. This proved not to be true. Being from the Middle East and a Moslem, I painfully learned that my challenges and obstacles were much greater than those of immigrants from other countries. I attended graduate school at the University of Wyoming, receiving my Master of Science degree in 1969. I continued my education at the University of Northern Colorado and Denver University, studying for a doctoral degree in Educational Administration.

Because of the constant turmoil in the Middle East and the uncertainty of a promising future in Iran, I had no intention of going back. I was unhappy living under the dictatorship of the late Shah, and I could not disagree more with the unpleasant conditions that the present Islamic government has created for its citizens. Therefore, I purposely took my time, prolonging my studies and practical training to stay in America. I worked hard to earn my citizenship. The fortunate ones, who need only be born on U.S. soil to be granted this citizenship, should be appreciative of the great gift given to them at birth. We have a precious life in America and should be very thankful.

I applied for and was awarded my certificate of naturalization in 1980 in Denver, Colorado. At last, I was a free man able to enjoy a life never possible in my old country.

Acceptance in America has not been easy for people from the Middle East. Most are given the stigma of "terrorists" because of terrorism around the world in recent years, and most particularly in our homeland with the heinous act of 9/11. These acts of terrorism are committed by a minority group of Moslem fundamentalists, constituting only one per cent of the entire Islamic population. In most cases, their actions are a response to their interpretation of American foreign policies.

I am an American by choice and very proud of it. The fact that some immigrants give priority to their old country versus their newly adopted nation seriously troubles me. They should be grateful for the many opportunities which they have now but did not have in their former country. Regardless of our religion or the country we came from, as immigrants we must consider the future of our new country more important than that of the one we left.

People study second languages for various reasons, such as, vacationing in foreign countries, communication for ordering a beer, asking directions to the toilets, and other simple desires. Learning another language proficiently, to move to a new country, completing graduate school, or competing in the work place are enormous challenges. Therefore, earning a degree in a foreign language to pursue a career is an even more monumental task and often quite frustrating. Writing a book in a second language is a major accomplishment, and being published is, of course, the ultimate reward!

This book describes my continual struggle to achieve a livelihood to make a successful life in a new country. It has not been easy and certainly not the fairy tale which most immigrants, myself included, thought it would be. Often the road was quite painful; however, I kept reminding myself I had no country to return to. This was it! I am greatful that I did.

THE MAKING OF PARVIZ

Children in Iran do not have laws or agencies to protect them from abuse. Four out of five children in Palestine, Iraq and Afghanistan do not have shoes. They have nothing to do with terrorism, but because of the stigma given to their country by American and world politicians, they have generally been excluded from receiving help.

We in America are becoming numb and accustomed to news reports and special TV programs concerning heartbreaking, inhumane child abuse cases around the world. For example, in April 1996 the television show "Justice Files" ran a documentary on Russian orphanages in which children were administered drugs. This was done to keep them controllable so they could be placed in factories to perform the menial labor tasks that other Russians would not do. Haitian children are routinely kidnapped and taken to the Dominican Republic. There they are forced to work on sugar farms under the most horrible conditions. Some of these countries do not allow reporters to publicize such crimes against children.

During the eight-year war with Iraq (1980-1988), Iran was even more guilty of child abuse. Thousands of children lost their lives or were injured on the battlefields. The Ayatollah Khomeini promised their parents that the children would be given the key to heaven if they were martyrs for the cause. These innocent, poor sacrificial youngsters were forced to walk before the troops, thereby discharging the mines set by Saddam Hussein's invading army. This assured the safety of the soldiers following behind the children.

Sadly, many of these victimized children did not die, but lost their limbs. Those who have lost their legs are often left with only one option to get around, and that is cutting a part of a rubber tire, tying it to their waist and then lifting themselves with their arms to scoot from one place to another. Wheelchairs are not easily available in Iran, and most of these children, who now are in their mid thirties and without money, have no other option.

I would like to see more aggressive movements in all nations, particularly third world countries, to protect children from abuse. Many heads of states, their spouses, celebrities, and others have created a number of fund raising projects to improve the living conditions for children throughout the world. I admire their outstanding human compassion in this worthy cause. Unfortunately, children of the Middle East thus far have not been included in their plans. The former Princess Diana of Britain and Hillary Rodham Clinton, while she was the first lady, supported many humanitarian efforts for children. However, for political reasons Middle Eastern children, like those in Iran, were excluded.

My own childhood was marred by constant parental abuse. My father, Nader, was an employee of Bank Melli, the national bank of Iran in Tabriz, a cosmopolitan city in western Iran near the Turkish border. He was an intelligent, gifted man, who spoke seven languages fluently. Musically talented, he played the Iranian sitar, flute, and piano. He was a handsome man, who possessed the charm attributed to many Persian males, a true ladies' man. However, as a father he was a complete failure. He drank heavily, smoked opium, had numerous affairs, and was very self-centered. He physically, emotionally, and verbally abused us.

My mother, Rosa, a name given to her when she attended the American High School in Tabriz, was petite and beautiful, with big brown eyes. She also was the daughter of a wealthy and protective father. As was typical of her generation, my mother's marriage was arranged by her father. She was 16 years old. Her husband was fifteen years older. Rosa never seemed to mature mentally beyond her teenage years, as her knowledge of love, affection, sex, and responsibilities as a mother were quite child-like.

I am told by my older siblings that my parents had quite a nice, spacious home and comfortable family life when I came into the world. I was their fourth and last child. Sadly, I never knew the comforts of a loving and caring family, because my mother left when I was two years old. I was far too young to understand; however, my childhood memories are imprinted in my heart and soul forever.

The morning Rosa left was utter chaos. My parents were shouting, screaming, and my mother was packing while two strong men were moving Persian carpets out of the house. Rosa was crying. I remember running after her down the street. She turned around and slapped me so hard across the face that I fell in a heap on the ground crying. This is the haunting and crushing memory that my mother left me

Within a week of my mother's leaving, my father married Ozra, his young, buxom, flirtatious mistress. She had all the tools necessary to keep Nader to herself. An expert cook and eager sexual partner, she found my father's children to be an annoyance. Neglecting us out of jealousy and hatred, we were often left hungry and unwashed. I spent my childhood years in a home without parental love, kindness, warmth, compassion, or understanding. I was hurt, frightened, and lonely.

My two older sisters told me that a few months after my mother deserted us, my wicked stepmother, Ozra, left me naked in a snow bank. I was two and a half years old, too small to be able to open our heavy back door by myself. It was a cold winter night and she conveniently arranged an evening at the movies with my father. That night my sisters and brother could not find me. Looking everywhere, they all began to assume the worst. Children were often found drowned either accidentally or intentionally in the cement water tanks, called *ab-anbar*, located underneath the house. That was the first place they looked. Later that night my sister Ziba, frantic and desperate, found me outside, blue and barely breathing. Giving me warm milk, she put me in a tub of warm water and kept rubbing my cold hands and feet.

Every night after that, Ziba and I would cuddle together, keeping each other warm. She would tell me bedtime stories

3

until I fell asleep. Her soft voice and interesting stories form the basis of the few good memories of my childhood.

This terrifying event brought our wonderful, sweet grandmother Tala into my life. My older sister Layla and brother Reza went to her, begging for help. They told grandma how mean and unkind our stepmother was. She suggested we tell our father, but they explained that he would never believe us. Our father was so infatuated with his young bride that we were totally forgotten. Grandma Tala was shocked to learn that he never took time to talk to us, and our only communication with him was through the closed bathroom door. Layla, with her special charm and sincerity, was able to convince grandma that she was our only hope.

Tala was one of my grandfather Hakim's three wives, his first and the oldest. Naturally, this made the two younger wives more desirable to him. My grandfather was a successful surgeon in Iran, easily affording his several wives. Each wife had her own home, a car with a personal chauffeur, and numerous maids. Our loving grandmother wanted to take care of us in her spacious, luxurious home; however, our selfish grandfather forbade it. Devising a plan, she came to us two of the three alternating weeks, reserving the one required week for her husband.

This made my father very angry. He did not want his mother, nor his children, in his home. He suggested we be sent to an orphanage. Grandma Tala would not allow it, being well aware of the horrible conditions in those places.

Life in Iranian orphanages was so degrading and humiliating that most children would rather be dead. The sexual abuse had no age limit, starting as young as four or five years old, and it didn't matter whether you were a boy or girl. By the time a child reached the age of ten, this young person was trained in how to satisfy not only the personnel in charge but, also at times, everyone in the place: cooks, custodians, anyone else who could get away with it. The physical abuse was even worse. Children as young as a year old were found with broken bones.

Grandma Tala insisted she be allowed to take care of us. Her son finally agreed, giving us the large storeroom in the back of the house, but clothes and food were not a part of the agreement, as our uncaring father and stepmother gave us absolutely nothing.

Life with my grandmother was full of love, warmth, and wisdom. We had very few material comforts, but we were happy. Grandma Tala was our sole caretaker, both emotionally and financially. She did the best she could, bringing rice, cheese, bread, fruit, and occasionally milk and eggs from her home. She repeatedly asked her husband if she could take us to her own home. Cold-hearted as my grandfather was, he refused to grant her permission.

Culturally in most Asian countries a woman's role in life is subservient to a man's; therefore, she has no authority on her own to bring us to her home. We often went without food, but grandma's physical presence was more nurturing. She was our entire world, our security blanket, our protector, mentor, and teacher. She was everything to us!

Grandma made a home for us out of that old storeroom. She organized that one room into sections for us to sleep, play, study, and eat. She was a brilliant woman, teaching us about life and what was really important. She taught us not to dwell on material things in life, but to strive for mental accomplishments.

Tala made us believe that at the end of the day, what or how much we put in our stomachs did not matter as most of it would go to waste down the toilet. She told us that what we put in our brains and in our hearts is what really counts. This could never be taken away.

When I was about six years old, I went into the kitchen where Ozra had a large box of cherries. She used to make a variety of delicious things with them. One was a wonderful dinner with rice, meatballs, and cherries, called *Albaloo Polo.* She also used them to make a spicy liqueur with vodka for my father, called *Vishnoka.* Of course, we were never allowed to touch anything; yet those ripe red cherries were so tempting. My mouth was watering and I could just about taste them. I sneakily grabbed a fistful in my tiny hand, as she was no where in sight.

Suddenly she walked in on me and saw the cherries in my hand, shouting, "You little brat! What are you doing with my cherries?"

"Nothing," I replied, holding my hands behind me. Screaming at me that I was a liar, she slapped and kicked me hard, knocking me to the kitchen floor. I wet my pants, and even worse on *her* kitchen floor, which made her so angry that she would not stop kicking me.

The ruckus drew my sisters and brother into the kitchen. They were upset, seeing her viciously beating me. In a split second, the three of them instinctively pulled me away from her. Pushing her to the floor, Ziba held her by her long hair; Reza held her feet, and Layla took a broomstick, hitting her while I kept spitting on her face. We were a bunch of angry, frustrated children finally having revenge on our stepmother.

Afterwards, the four of us feared for our lives, wondering what would happen when Ozra told our father. We hid for the rest of the day and throughout the night. Much to our surprise, nothing happened! Either she was deeply embarrassed, not wanting to tell him, or she simply did not want to deal with it.

In any case, after that incident, we recognized our strength as a team. We discovered a power that we never knew existed before, and which we gleefully used several times throughout the years to battle this evil witch. From that moment on, her physical hostility toward us was tempered.

Later, in another cherry incident, we learned how to get Ozra in trouble with our father. She cleverly used to draw a line on her jars of cherry liqueur to mark their fullness. She was sure this method would alert her if anyone tampered with the liquid. What she didn't count on was our being more clever than she was. After all, we were starving children. We would eat some cherries, replace the juice with water up to the line, or simply draw a new line exactly like hers, erasing the old one.

Months later, after the liqueur had fermented, our father would zestfully open the jar, taking a big swallow in great anticipation of his favorite drink, only to gulp a watered down cherry liqueur. He would spit it out and become very angry, throwing the jar and its contents at Ozra or out the window. This was always followed by a shouting match. "What is wrong with you? Can't you make a simple drink anymore?" Rudely, she would throw something back at him, calling him names in return.

Almost every night my father would get drunk, and we would wait for the fighting to begin. Sometimes it was entertaining and better than the movies. The profanities would bounce back and forth between the two, along with any object they could get their hands on. Often their fights seemed funny, but we were also always frightened, not knowing what would happen next. Sometimes, either during or after the fight, my father would grab and beat one or all of us for not helping him. On other occasions, he would hit us, accusing us of interfering in his personal affairs. He never needed a justification. Our father would beat us if we had done something; he would beat us if we had not. The tragedy here is that, in all honesty, the four of us were very good children, never doing anything to warrant such brutal punishment. The beatings eventually became a regular, daily pattern, which we learned to deal with, each in our own way.

After awhile we knew the routine of how the evening would progress. When my father became drunk, the first thing he would do was complain about the taste of the food. Depending on Ozra's response, he would start shouting profanity, accusing her of being incapable of making a decent meal. If she could not calm him down, the next thing we knew, a plate of delicious food would go flying out the window. Luckily, this was one way for us to eat. Like a professional baseball team, the four of us would skillfully cover the yard. The goal was to quickly catch the plate like a fly ball, empty the food into a

7

bag, then break the plate and run. We had to break the plate so that my father would not wonder what had happened to his toss. By the time they would look out the window, we had disappeared. We would find a safe hiding place where we fairly divided the food among us. I still am amazed at how amicable four hungry children could be.

We were still living in Tabriz and I was in first grade when I saw my mother Rosa again. In the school yard, my siblings introduced a nicely dressed lady to me as *Mama*. I remember staring at her for a long time with disbelief and distrust, asking myself if this could really be my mother!

Some years later, father was transferred to Tehran, a move which totally changed our living situation. Tala thought a move and change would be good for us. Our future was so important to her that she chose to live permanently with us, not letting anyone know how uncomfortable she was about leaving her own nice home and affluent husband. The four of us had total trust in Tala's judgment and believed that Tehran, even with father and Ozra, meant bigger and better opportunities. Tala made us very excited about the move. The thought of living in Tehran, with all its glamour and possibilities, filled our heads with endless fantasies of a better life! I was now eight years old.

Our apartment in Tehran was not a big one. Two bedrooms, a large kitchen, dining room, and a makeshift living room were all connected by a long hallway. Although the apartment had a room with a sink and toilet, it did not have a bathtub or shower. Every other week or once a month, depending on our father's mood, we all went to a public bathhouse, about a fifteen minute walk away.

Our fourth-floor apartment took up the entire top floor of the building. The other floors had two apartments side by side. Although the apartment itself was too small for all seven of us, it had a large, open deck which we loved. Here we had the space to play and enjoyed a great view of the city. For father's convenience, our apartment was located in the crowded downtown area close to the national bank. This afforded us a wonderful nighttime view of twinkling lights and flashing neon signs which amused us endlessly.

Several years after we moved to Tehran, my grandfather Hakim passed away. My father and grandmother expected to come into a large fortune. Unfortunately, their inheritance was not nearly as much as hoped for. Because of the inequality of women in Iran, my grandfather's three wives and seven children, and no written will, his estate took longer than usual to distribute. It was months before Grandma received her share. It wasn't much, but she was happy to have any amount to spend for our food, clothing, school supplies, and other necessities.

Using his charm and cunning ways, my father managed to borrow all of Tala's inheritance, opening a photo shop and stationery store. Lending the money to him in good faith, she thought additional income from her son's business would improve our living conditions. Her optimism was reinforced by his assurance of monthly payments with good interest. The investment, however, never made a profit. The stationery store was neglected due to the overtime commitment to his job at the bank, coupled with his drinking habits, which made the venture a total failure.

Money became a continuous source of argument between my father and grandmother. However, with or without money, she was a tireless source of inspiration for us in our lives and education. Her reward was our performance in school, where we all were top students in our classes, consistently receiving straight A's. Her inability to get money from her son to support us was the most distressing factor in Grandma Tala's life.

Shortly after this, father and Ozra had a baby daughter, Nina. My grandmother, my sisters, plus my brother and I shared one bedroom. Father and his new family occupied the rest of the apartment. A kerosene stove was placed in the room to both warm us and cook our food. We were in a new city, but

9

back to the old understanding of never stepping foot in their territory. We could not expect to eat with them or even receive leftover table scraps from their meals. The only time we saw our father was when he used the toilet, which was in our section of the apartment. If we needed to talk to him, once again it was through this closed door.

Watching from the outdoor deck or the hallway, we could see my father and his family dining on delicious food. The tantalizing aroma filled the room and made our tummies rumble. We ran to our Grandma, begging and crying, telling her how hungry we were. In her own clever way she would stop our tears by pretending to cook for us. Gracefully and determinedly she would turn on the kerosene stove, placing a pot of water with a few rocks in it on top of the stove. The clanking of the rocks as she stirred fooled us into thinking she was cooking real food. She would continue to patiently stir and, with time, we became so tired we fell asleep, forgetting our empty bellies. The next morning with wide-eyes we would ask her, "What happened to our meal?" She would gently tell us that relatives or friends had visited that evening, and, as is the traditional Persian custom, she had to serve the food to the guests. We never doubted Grandma; our trust was unquestioning.

My grandmother was a chain-smoker, and often I would find her quietly crying to herself. She no longer could afford to purchase cigarettes, and my father would not buy them for her. Watching her simply broke my heart. One day Ziba and I went out into the street searching for discarded cigarette butts. This hurt her pride tremendously; however, she had no other choice, and she always graciously accepted our little gifts.

The one bright spot and place in our lives was the huge wrap-around deck off the hallway. We spent much of our free time there, especially during the hot summer months. Sometimes we even took our blankets and pillows and slept under the stars.

One warm evening, as we often did, we decided to climb, jump, and skip from one roof top to the other to watch the movie at the outdoor theater down the block.

From where we were perched on the fifth floor, one of us accidentally knocked a piece of rock down onto the audience, hitting a bald man on the head and creating quite a commotion and panic. Everyone gathered around the profusely bleeding man forcing the theater owners to stop the movie. Being young kids, we thought it was funny, yet we were terrified, thinking what would happen when father found out. Taking off as fast as we could, we scrambled from roof top to roof top and at home hid under our blankets. Frightened and feeling guilty, we stayed away from our secret movie place for a long time.

Our miserable lives were a constant strain for Grandma, causing her health to deteriorate. She could never understand why her son treated his children so cruelly. The daily worry of not being able to provide us with basic necessities, especially school books and supplies, which parents are expected to purchase, only exacerbated her illness.

In the middle of the night, vomiting blood and crying helplessly, Grandma Tala became terribly sick. She could not even get out of bed. Her moaning woke us up, frightening us terribly. Being young children, we were helpless and began crying with her. This was the first time we saw our grandmother desperate, devoid of her usual pride and dignity.

A decision had to be made and it fell on the shoulders of my thirteen-year old brother, Reza, because Layla was busy attending to grandma.

Reza was the book-worm of the family. Smart, shy, and quiet, unlike the rest of us, he was not a dare-devil or aggressive at all. Usually, my oldest sister, Layla, had to fight his battles.

Of average height with dark hair and brown eyes, his talent was making toys. He could make cars and trucks out of simple cardboard and trash, and then he would sell them for a little pocket money. In the 1940's in Tehran, there were not many toys on the market for children. I remember a few of his handmade trucks were so nearly perfect that people would make high bids to purchase them. Another source of income for him was selling homework to other students. His best sellers were mathematics, drafting, art, and science projects. Since he was so mechanically inclined, he also made additional income by repairing appliances for people of the neighborhood.

Violating all the household rules, Reza walked down the long hallway and crossed the off limits boundary, knocking on father's bedroom door. There was no answer. He pounded again, yelling hysterically. Nader got out of bed, swearing loudly. Pulling on his pants, he opened the door to see what all the commotion was about. Following Reza to our end of the house, he took one look at his mother, and he was wide awake. He was scared and frightened; none of us had to explain anything to him. He ran back to his bedroom, putting on his shoes and jacket to take her to the hospital. We all helped carry her slight body down the long flights of stairs. Once outside we hailed a taxi, leaving father and Reza to take her to a hospital.

Public hospitals, administered by the government, were dreadful and nothing like you have ever seen. A room with a capacity for eighteen patients would normally have about forty beds squeezed in it. Beds were also placed in hallways and entryways. Patients were so packed together that it was not unusual for a dead person to go unnoticed for two or three days. Only a person with absolutely no other alternative would admit himself to a public hospital. Staff, who were supposedly obligated to provide the most basic supplies, would steal the medicines for resale to patients. Ironically, cooks, doormen, drivers, janitors, and other support staff outnumbered doctors and nurses 5 to 1. It wasn't unusual to see gardeners on staff where there was no garden. It also wasn't unusual to see the cook take the best cuts of meat, rice, vegetables, and fruits home for either his family or to sell on the black market. As a consequence, the patients often were served the poorest quality food and the cook had one of the nicest homes on the block. Needless to say, his superiors' wallets were also padded. The whole system was so corrupt.

People who could afford it went to private hospitals where

the care and service was far superior.

All this was occurring during the Shah's well-known, but misleading, campaign advertising to the world how modern Iran was becoming. Today, with economic sanctions causing runaway inflation and medicine being scarce, I cannot begin to imagine the state of those hospitals!

Once, I, myself, had to be treated in a public hospital after having been in a jeep accident involving two of my teachers and three other students. Nearing my home, we must have taken a corner too quickly because suddenly the jeep flipped over. Although the injuries were not serious, there was a lot of blood. Witnesses thought that we all were dead or certainly would not survive. Somehow, miraculously, sitting in the back between one of the teacher's and a fellow student, I was not hurt. Since I was not injured, I was the first one out of the jeep. The neighbors, who did not see me getting out, thought I was crushed under the car. One of them ran to my house, telling Ozra I had been killed in a car accident; but instead I was in an ambulance along with the rest of my companions. After being released from the hospital, I returned home.

When Ozra opened the door she had a big smile on her face, believing that she was finally rid of me. Seeing me at the door and thinking I had returned as a ghost to seek revenge and haunt her for the rest of her life, she passed out. Thus, we had to take her to the same dilapidated hospital for treatment.

Several weeks went by and we were missing our grandmother terribly. We continuously begged our father to take us to visit her, and each day he would promise to take us the following day. The next day would come and he would have another excuse. When he ran out of excuses, he told us that he had just learned that visitors under the age of eighteen were not allowed in that hospital. He assured us, however, that grandma was doing well and would be home soon. Later we found out everything he said was a lie. Father had never gone to see her.

Layla was a very pretty girl with a medium build, green eyes, and brown hair. With her knack for creative art and

13

homemaking, we often viewed her as our mother. Washing, mending, and altering our clothes, she always made sure we looked decent. Occasionally, old clothes were given to us by neighbors or friends. With her sewing skills, she would make them look like new. One of her greatest talents was making clothes from anything she could find. Old curtains, sheets, or remnants people threw out were sufficient for her to design an entire wardrobe for us. She even made extra money by sewing and altering clothes for others.

One day Layla came up with a brilliant plan that got us all excited. She suggested that we should try to find our Uncle Abi, a pre-med student, who lived in a university dormitory in northwest Tehran. We were confident that he would be able to take us to Grandma Tala's hospital to visit her, and maybe even bring her home.

Uncle Abi expressed his desire to help us. The next day he came to take us to the hospital. He also was able to convince father, his stepbrother, to come along. By this time three months had passed since we had last seen grandma. We were overwhelmed with excitement at the idea of bringing her home. Layla helped get us ready. She washed us, combed our hair, shined our shoes and pressed our clothes in preparation for the hospital visit. We patiently waited for father who took his sweet time getting ready. The excitement of bringing Grandma Tala home was overwhelming!

What we found out at the hospital made our hearts stop. Imagine our shock upon hearing that our grandmother had died nine days after admittance, lonely and by herself. We could not believe our ears. I never forgave my father!

Nader further complicated the situation by incorrectly stating her family records on her admittance forms. The hospital supervisor told Uncle Abi they had sincerely tried to contact the next of kin, but with no luck. Against hospital regulations, her body had been kept in the morgue for three weeks in hopes of finding a relative or friend for a proper, religious burial. The supervisor kept thinking that a family member would be stopping by to visit Grandma Tala. He was surprised that no one did. He explained to us that they had no choice but to bury her in an unmarked grave in the city cemetery, where the homeless and indigent were buried. He further told us that grandma was too ill and could not communicate with the staff; yet, it was evident from her manners that she was a lady of class, not a homeless person. He then took us into his office and gave us her death certificate and, thereby, we learned the location of her grave.

Words cannot begin to describe our grief and pain. As young as I was, the nightmare was even worse - she was my protector, nurturer, my everything. Every night I cried secretly, my head buried underneath the blanket. For months, even years after her death, the thought of never seeing her again would send me into deep sobs. She was and still is the most influential and motivating person in my life. Grandma's commonly used phrases and tireless advice were instrumental in making me the person I am today. One favorite saying of hers provided me with a great deal of comfort: *There will always be bright, warm, sunny daylight even after the darkest, coldest, blackest night.* For me, she was that bright morning sun. She was my life.

After she passed away, life became even harder. The constant battle for food with father and Ozra continued. Meanwhile, Layla married our cousin Abbas, escaping the woeful living conditions we had to continue to endure. Also, by this time, my natural mother had married a Russian soldier from Azerbaijan. She had a new family, bearing him a son and daughter. Later, for political reasons, he returned to Russia taking his children and leaving my mother, for her own personal reasons, in Iran.

Shortly afterward, Reza left home to become a chemical engineer for the largest petroleum refinery in Iran. Passing a difficult exam, he was one of twenty-five elite high school graduates admitted to a British-based college in Abadan, called Abadan Oil Technical College. There he received a superb free college education with substantial monthly allowances.

Now it was up to Ziba to raise me. She stepped into the void and became my protector and guide, although by this time I was adept at taking care of myself.

Ziba was slim, of medium height, with striking blue eyes and dark hair. Incredibly beautiful both physically and mentally, we called her the Elizabeth Taylor of Iran. Combining strength and maturity rare for her tender age of thirteen, she developed into an exceptional human being. Her ability to handle pressure under the most intolerable, deplorable conditions was always amazing to me. She became my second mother.

Something that always astounded me was her ability to bravely pick up a burning charcoal with her bare hands. She did this to demonstrate her emotional and mental strength. "It all has to do with your state of mind," she told me. I now know it was mind over matter. With her charming voice and pleasant ways, I was captivated by Ziba.

When I was in the fourth grade, I suddenly became seriously ill, and a doctor diagnosed my irregular heart beat as an incurable heart condition. The doctor told me I had perhaps only three months to live and confided in my father that I must refrain from any kind of physical activity; otherwise, my death could be hastened. This made me very sad because I had always dreamed of being a soccer player.

During this period, penicillin shots had to be administered every two hours, around the clock, for the first ninety days. Father gave me the shots, but the bad part was that Ziba had to wake him up each time. If she couldn't wake him up, I went without my medication. As a result Ziba took on the task, learning to give me the shots herself. She thought this would be easier than trying to wake up my father each time; thus, she became not only my surrogate mother but also my personal nurse.

Months went by. Instead of dying I became stronger and stronger. Ziba missed three months of school to stay home and take care of me. As the weeks progressed, my fever subsided

16

and I was able to slowly move around. Against all odds Ziba managed to give me the nutrition necessary to recuperate. She did this by stealing food from the wooden cupboard where Ozra locked her supplies.

My recovery took more than a year, leaving me bedridden for the first six months. It took the next six months to rid my body of the strong medication which made me very hyper and also caused me to lose my sense of balance, walking like a drunk.

One day I found an old tennis ball and it became my salvation. Dribbling and maneuvering the ball with my feet, it went everywhere with me. In the city I dribbled around dogs, trees, and through gutters called *jube*. Cars, trucks, and motorcycles were no obstacles as I maneuvered that ball across the streets with my feet. Considering the traffic in Tehran, this new-found sport was taking my life in my hands. Oblivious to the dangers, I transformed the honking horns and crazy traffic noises into the cheering fans and athletic triumphs of my dreams. I imagined myself as the greatest soccer star, playing to a sold-out crowd in Tehran's only stadium, *Amjadiyeh.* Everyone was cheering for me in a big international soccer match.

I easily made the decision of secretly signing up with a soccer club a short distance away. I thought, if I am going to die, it is not going to make much difference if I die a little earlier, so I may as well run and play soccer. Obviously, the regular workouts, contrary to outdated medical theories, made me stronger and healthier. I continued to improve without dropping dead, as the doctor had expected.

Needless to say, I could not tell anyone in the family of my training. They would have stopped me, never allowing me to play. Not even for a day.

Ziba was fifteen years old when father and Ozra forced her to marry Ali, a 48-year-old medical school student who was Ozra's nephew. Ziba was infatuated with a nice young police officer, with no intentions of marrying the older man. She did

17

everything she could to change our father's mind; however, her attempts were unsuccessful as they continued to pressure her. To prove her seriousness, she attempted suicide twice, once slitting her wrists with my father's razor, the second time by ingesting an enormous amount of sleeping pills leftover from my medications. Both times she was saved by Ali's tireless effort. He was intent on saving the life of his future wife. Against her wishes, she married him shortly afterward, and they moved into their new apartment.

Because of father's growing family, we moved from the old apartment to a house. My father was able to purchase a larger home from the sale of his stationery store and the inheritance left to him by his mother.

With Ziba's marriage, I was the only one left at home to be the punching bag, and I had just turned fourteen years of age. By now, my father and Ozra had two more children, Susan and Ahmad. For me, the difficulty was no longer the physical abuse but watching the five of them eat right in front of me. Smelling the delectable Persian food and not being able to partake of it was the worst possible torture for a growing teenage boy. I would be smacked if I either got close to their dining table, or even looked at them while they were eating. Father and Ozra claimed that watching them while they ate made them feel uncomfortable and took their appetite away.

I continued doing well in school. Because of my academic scores and athletic accomplishments, I was a very popular student. In the Iranian educational system, contrary to what we have in the United States, there is no middle school. After completing six years of elementary schooling, students would go directly to high school. Because of my advance skills in controlling a soccer ball, I was able to become a starting varsity player in seventh grade. As a ninth grader, I was the highest scoring player on the varsity soccer team.

I matured into a strong and muscular young man, with the same beautiful blue eyes as my sister Ziba, uncommon for most Persians. This made me very handsome to the ladies. I continued to be very athletic and also had a natural talent for making money.

In addition to a love for singing and dancing, I also was a practical joker and derived much pleasure out of making people smile. It was my way of escaping reality and immersing myself in a world full of laughter and fun.

When I was with Layla, Reza, Ziba and their families, I was always the center of attention. These were happy times for me and helped me forget the agony of my day to day life at home. Making light of the sadness that was etched in my heart was a unique gift I had and my way of coping.

One of the things I liked to do best was mimic other people. Of course, imitating father and Ozra gave me the most enjoyment, and made my sisters and brothers roll on the floor with laughter. I also liked to imitate the mullahs, the soccer coach, our principal, the politicians, popular singers, and the street vendors.

During recess, I would earn my lunch money by charging the other students 25 *rials* for doing impromptu stand-up comedy, mimicking teachers, staff, and the principal. Thank goodness I wasn't caught by the faculty!

I've always kept my sense of humor, and because of it, I was very popular with all my cousins, nieces, and nephews.

My athletic accomplishments made me sought after by my fellow students. Many times the only way for me to eat lunch in high school was to challenge the affluent students in basketball, a source of entertainment for them. I would bet them that I could score a basket using only my head or my feet. No one could believe I could do it, as most of the rich kids in our school could barely score baskets with their hands. They forfeited their lunch or some money if I was successful. Without being immodest, I must admit that I ate well!

Kids in my neighborhood were very proud of me. Instead of introducing me as a varsity soccer player, they would brag and say that I was a member of the "National Team," which was a tremendous boost to my ego. One day all these

19

exaggerations caused a serious dilemma for me, creating one of the most unforgettable soccer experiences of my life.

Kids, who had lost their money to a bully from a different neighborhood close by came begging for help. He was a goal keeper, betting the youngsters that they could not score against him. One by one the boys tried but could not make a goal, losing all their money. Putting their heads together, they came up with a plan to win their money back, double or nothing. They wanted me to kick for them. They were so adamant that I could not refuse. If I did, I probably would not be able to live on the same street with them.

I decided to forget about a fancy shot. I would just kick the ball with all my strength, so even if the goal keeper caught the ball, he would be thrown backwards into the goal. The place for the challenge was set up in a little side alley opening to a main alley, forming a T. I was to kick from the middle of the side alley, approximately 15 yards, to the goal. Not knowing where the soccer ball would go if the goal keeper didn't catch it, I kicked it with all my might. The bully was too slow to react. Joyfully the boys were jumping up and down screaming for their money back. Meanwhile, in the main alley, an old lady in her *chador* was shuffling by. A *chador* is a large, square cloth traditionally worn as a shawl or cloak by Moslem women. It is draped over the top of the head and then grasped with one hand under the chin. My ball hit the poor lady and I saw loaves of bread (*sangak*), a *chador*, a bowl, fresh yogurt, and a woman flying in the air. I thought, what have I done? Scared to death, I ran to the end of the side alley, climbed a straight wall to a roof, and hid until everyone was gone.

The woman's family came out, beating every kid who was there, not listening to their protests. The boys kept yelling, "Parviz did it! Parviz did it!" No one believed them since I was too good a player to spend my time in the streets with these kids. Later, we found out that the old lady was all right, no broken bones, just badly shaken up with a few bruises.

I also had the uncanny talent of making more money from

any little amount I could get my hands on. Being able to turn twenty five *rials* into fifty by betting, reinvesting, buying, or selling things learned in my early years became a valuable tool for me throughout my life, especially in my struggles to become successful in Iran and later in America. Otherwise, one of my options as an adult in the old country was to be a vendor of sunglasses or some other common profession. If not for this talent, I could still be living on welfare or working from paycheck to paycheck.

Not having enough to eat and vigorously training as a member of the Junior National Soccer Team was increasingly arduous. Comfort in my life had been nonexistent for most of the time. The basic necessities of food, school supplies, and clothing were becoming increasingly more difficult to acquire. My soccer achievements with supportive fans were the bright spots of my life. Fortunately, many times my teammates took me to their homes, where their wonderful mothers cooked many delicious dinners. If not for their kindness, I would not have had a decent meal.

Another blessing given to me was the thoughtful neighbors on our street, who knew of my situation and found me to be a polite and likable teenager. Some of the women would hide under their *chador* small plates of their delicious cooking and baking. Their generosity made my appalling home life more bearable.

But I could not depend all the time on the charity of others, and I knew that on my own I would have to come up with some way of feeding myself. As my family was not poor, there was plenty of food in our own kitchen! This is what I did:

1) One of my household chores was to buy bread, fruit, cheese, milk, and eggs on a daily basis for the family. I did this by signing a credit slip which Nader paid twice a month with his paycheck. On my own, I decided to buy a little bit extra, eating it in the street before I reached home.

2) I kept a keen eye on Ozra, watching where she hid the leftovers so that I could steal some later. Sadly, that did not

happen often as they consumed most of their meals.

3) I knew Ozra would always turn out the lights so that I would not see her hiding the food. But I was more clever and more desperate, and I observed her every move. Sometimes I would scare her by talking to her in her deceased aunt's voice. She would think that her aunt's ghost was in the house, drop the food, which I would grab and run. A couple of times she fainted out of sheer fright. I quickly learned that this was not the best of plans, as she later learned it was me, and I would receive a severe beating from Nader. No love was lost in that family. What I did was merely a desperate act to survive when no other choice was available.

Because of my grandmother's nurturing us and implanting the seed in our minds that we must develop our potential to be the best that we can be, my siblings and I were able to make a success of our lives. We eventually earned enough money to get by, had clothes to wear, something to eat, toys to play with, our own home entertainment at night, and a strong spirit to overcome our many disadvantages. We surely made the best of the little we had!

While writing this book, and reflecting on my past, something came to mind that I had never before thought about. And that was how the four of us never fought or argued, and how we had a very special bond and closeness.

The other was that my father never abused Nina, Susan, or Ahmad. I wondered then, and still do, why he treated us so differently. It always seemed so unfair! Perhaps it was because he was afraid of Ozra, who would kill him if he mistreated her children. Perhaps abusing the four of us was all he could handle. I'll never know. Not understanding why my father didn't share with me the abundance of food, clothes, and affection his new family was given deeply hurt me.

In later years, as an adult and still living in Iran, I had little contact with any of them. No one came to my wedding, nor was any one of them invited. My first child was born in Tehran without any congratulations or acknowledgment on their part. I completely lost track of them when I left for America. It was many years later, with the help of Layla, that I learned of the whereabouts of my half sisters and half brother.

Shortly after the Islamic Revolution of 1979, Susan and her family fled to The Netherlands as political refugees. Nina, Ahmad, and their respective families also left Iran and live comfortably in London.

In the summer of 1996, I traveled to Europe, making a special effort to find them with the hopes of beginning new relationships. The reunion was a heartwarming success. I enjoyed their families and their hospitality; they were very kind to my American wife, Angelica, and me, making us feel welcomed. Being in their company at last gave me answers and some sort of closure to my past.

It also brought back many memories of my marvelous grandmother. Her meaningful advice, attention, and coaching returned to me as if it were only yesterday.

I cried during the entire plane trip home from Europe. It was as if my grandmother were with me once again. It really felt as if I were seeing her and talking to her for one last time. My lovely wife was concerned for me, not knowing what I was going through. All the suppressed feelings which I had buried deep in my heart for more than 50 years came spilling out in tears. I was totally drained and exhausted when we landed.

Remembering some of grandmother Tala's meaningful and comforting philosophical points finally made me stop crying. Her words kept going around in my mind like a never ending tape. I have memorized them all for the rest of my life, but at this particular time I valued every single phrase even more. I would like to share some with you. Grandma Tala told me the following:

* Never expect life to be perfect. Often opportunities come at the wrong time or in the wrong place.
* When you have a "lady," you do not have a room, and when you have a place, you can't find a "lady." Don't

23

expect everything to be the way you want.

* Those who need attention, often are ignored; the ones who do not need it are smothered in affection.
* Those who need the most love are usually the hardest ones to give love to.
* When you are young and able to eat, you don't have the money to buy food. Then, when you are old and have money, often you have no appetite, teeth, or your health.
* People who are young and healthy often do not have the money to enjoy life. By the time they have money, they may not have their health or a partner to enjoy it with.
* The most beautiful flowers will grow and survive under the harshest conditions in the desert, under the rocks and in places where it would seem impossible to grow. The same is true for a person.
* You must disregard the unpleasant circumstances, never giving up hope, always reaching for the highest possible goal. If you succeed, it will be a dream come true. If you don't, your final stage will still be higher than the one from which you started.

I was 18 years old and a freshman in college when I saw my mother, Rosa, again. Her Russian husband had returned to Baku, Azerbaijan, taking their two children with him, and she was left homeless on the street. Living on a scholarship in one room rented from a family, I agreed to let her live with me. Without knowing or loving my mother, I supported her financially for 42 years until she passed away in February 2000 in Nashville, Tennessee.

I graduated from Teachers University in Tehran in 1961. My dream was to help children to become the best they could be. As a matter of fact, for many years, it was my dream to open an orphanage in Iran to give love and support to needy children, providing them with a comfortable home and someone who would love them. I wanted to follow Tala's valuable teaching methods to make these orphaned children strong, able

24

to ignore unpleasant situations, and to have happy lives. Devoting my life to children and making them successful was all I ever wanted to do. Because of political reasons, I never could return to Iran to fulfill my ambition; however, I am happy to say that I have achieved other goals. I have made significant differences in many children's lives by teaching and training thousands of youths to become successful athletes and adults.

Fortunately, I was a dreamer with a drive, willing to work hard, and gain a good education. Without financial resources but because of sports, grants, and professional positions, I was able to travel the world.

I can remember that when I was fourteen years old, I used to stand outside the stadium door, waiting to have a glimpse of the Iranian Olympic soccer players wanting to see what they looked like, how they dressed, and how they walked. Then, I would go home and practice and practice with my soccer ball until I could not stand up.

I can proudly say that all my workouts and dedication paid off, because when I turned nineteen I played on the same team with nine of these players. Later I had the privilege to travel to Europe and Asia to compete in international matches.

To my credit, I have earned national championships in soccer and track and field, and in the 1961 World University Games in Sofia, Bulgaria I was the only track and field competitor from Iran.

My friends who knew me well gave me the honorable title of "Champion Without Gold." I attained the highest level of my ability in sports and competed with top athletes from around the world, which made me very proud. It happened only because of being able to ignore the deplorable living conditions at home. Even when I was playing on the best soccer team in the nation, *Shahin,* life at home was still unbearable. I would like to share one father/son story which a good friend of mine, Mr. Diba, later told me.

One night I returned home from a strenuous soccer practice.

I went directly to my bedroom, which was in the basement and resembled a dungeon. My father came downstairs from his comfortable, luxurious living room to talk to me. I thought that he must have been waiting up for me. My heart started pounding as I said to myself, "What did I do wrong this time that he wants to punish me for?" I knew his bad mouthing would be followed by hitting, and then I wouldn't be able to study for my test the next day. Surprisingly, he was in a good mood and asked me in a pleasant manner, "Hey, big shot, with all your years of playing that silly game, you must know someone who can give us two free tickets to watch the match with the Russians this Friday." In Moslem countries, Friday is a holiday, or day of rest, and all important sports events are scheduled on that day, rather than Sundays, as scheduled in Western nations.

I was stunned to hear that Nader wanted to watch a soccer match and wondered if I had heard him correctly. He continued in his usual drunken state: "My colleagues at the bank have been talking about this game. They are all saying that the Dynamos are the best team in Russia. They said tickets are selling as high as six hundred *tomans* ($90.00 US dollars in 1960). "You know I wouldn't pay six *tomans* for one, but if you could get two free tickets, I will go with you. I don't want to go by myself."

I was amazed by Nader's sudden interest in going to a soccer match and couldn't help looking at him puzzled. But I responded, "Sure, I can get you free tickets for any game you want." Nader quickly replied, "I don't care to go to any other game. I just want to watch the Russians. Maybe I'll even have a chance to practice my Russian and talk to a few players or even the coach. You must come with me. I don't want to get lost in that goddamned stadium." I reached into my briefcase and handed him one of the sectional complimentary tickets which were given to us by the soccer federation for each game.

My father was shocked to have the ticket in his hand. He sarcastically said; "When did you rob the bank or did you win

26

the lottery? Where is yours? I told you that I won't go by myself." I showed him another ticket, saying, "I will not be able to go with you because of an important previous commitment, but you will not miss me, as these tickets are numbered." I assured him that it would not be possible for him not to see me there. Nader couldn't believe how many tickets I had for the game, nor how simple it was for him to obtain one.

He apparently found his seat by himself, but he became agitated because I wasn't there next to him. Looking around and cussing when the seats near him became occupied, his odd behavior attracted the attention of the spectators around him, particularly the gentleman, Mr. Diba, seated right next to him. He was my good friend, to whom I had given one of the complimentary tickets. This distinguished, middle-aged attorney was a serious soccer fan and always treated me as one of his family. Mr. Diba could not tolerate my father's restlessness and squirming around in his seat. He asked him, "Sir, are you looking for someone?"

"Yes, my goddamned son! He promised to be here," my father replied.

"What does your son look like? I'll help you look for him. This is a big stadium, and maybe his seat is in a different row." Then Nader gave Mr. Diba a description of me, followed by my first name. Mr. Diba thought that this man was joking. To be certain that he was thinking of the same person, he asked Nader for my last name. When my father said Emamian, Mr. Diba's mouth fell open. Nader said, " I can't stand his trickery any longer." "What kind of tricks?" Mr. Diba asked, thinking that he was sitting next to some sort of nut. He did not know what to make out of this strange conversation, never guessing that this off-the-wall man could possibly be my father.

Everyone in Iran knew Parviz Emamian, the soccer player. Naturally, he would be on the playing field and not sitting in the stadium. My friend believed that the man sitting next to him was either drunk or out of his mind, and it made him nervous. To play it safe he said to my father, "I don't think

27

your son tricked you, sir. If Parviz is who you are looking for, he is here and I promise you, you will see him. But tell me please, are you a soccer fan?"

"The hell I am! I hate the goddamned game. I just came this one time to watch the Russians play," Nader answered.

"Have you ever watched Parviz play?" Mr. Diba asked. Nader replied, "I can't even stand looking at him around the house, and I certainly don't care to watch him play soccer on the streets! Besides, what is so great about kicking around a dumb ball?"

Mr. Diba began putting the pieces together and realized that he indeed was my father. He then started to kid my father trying to make him feel a bit guilty, by saying, "Parviz is a very valuable player in our country. How could you not know this, if you are his father? I think you did the nicest thing that you could do for yourself by coming here today. I'm sure that you will never be sorry. You are going to witness something you have never seen in your entire life."

"Oh yeah, what do you mean by that?" asked Nader.

"Yes," said Mr. Diba, "you are going to watch your son play against the Russians. What do you think about that?"

"Are you kidding me?" Nader asked.

"No, sir, but I wish I were. Somehow I have a feeling you have not been much of a father or of significant help and inspiration to Parviz."

"You're right, I haven't. Come to think of it, Parviz didn't have any lunch today or supper last night that I know of," Nader said.

"Why?" Mr. Diba asked.

"Well, he and my wife don't get along. I try to stay out of it but I never dreamt that he could play in this kind of a match, or that he was good enough to play against the Russians. I would have given him my own lunch had I known. By the way, how well do you know my son?" Nader asked.

"Oh, I watch all his games; I admire him a lot, and I wish that any one of my children was like him. Well, it is too late to

28

worry about the lunch or dinner now, here come the players," said Mr. Diba, noticing that Nader had put his hands over his face in shame, feeling too guilty to watch his son enter the standing-room only stadium. He became so involved with his thoughts and his guilt that he missed the cheers and standing ovation for the players.

As the game progressed, spectators were going wild with each play. The moves and action were rapid. Every cheer and round of applause for me made my father cry in anguish and pain for all the things he never did for me. After the game, Nader, along with many fans, waited outside the locker room to praise the players for the excellent competition, disregarding the score and our loss to the Russian team.

I had to push my way through the crowd to get to my father. I just wanted to see his face. I was dying to see his behavior toward me after so many years of neglect and abuse. I hoped to hear his apology for never supporting me.

He invited me to dinner and drinks that night, telling me how he would try to change and make things up to me by trying to provide a better life. I told him, "Thanks, but no thanks."

That was the last time I dealt with my father, as I moved in with the Diba family and avoided seeing him at all costs. I have never forgiven him for not being a father to me.

Thinking about the neglect, the abuse, the suffering, and starvation I continuously endured throughout my childhood without parental support always makes me wonder how far I could have gone with a proper home, better environment, and caring parents. Maybe I could have been a World or Olympic champion! I will never know. This probably was the reason that my close, loving friends gave me the honor of calling me "Champion."

I owe my life to Ziba for keeping me alive during my illness, and all of my accomplishments are a tribute to the world's most exceptional coach and human being, my Grandmother Tala.

They have been taken from me and are now in heaven. May God bless their souls and keep them safe.

Family Post log

Later my siblings created interesting lives for themselves:

Layla, after having three children, completed her college degree specializing in creative homemaking. She conducted her own private school for women at home for many years. Her main talent was sewing, flower-making with fabrics and home decorations. She generated the same kind of effective inspiration in her students that she did in us. She now has four wonderful children, two boys and two girls, and six grandchildren.

After a lifetime of struggle, she and her husband retired. They wanted to immigrate to the United States, but because of the financial restrictions the Iranian government places on citizens who try to leave the country, it is monetarily impossible. Leaving substantial assets behind, my sister and her husband were permitted to exit Iran taking only $500 each. It was their wish to spend their last years in a free country, not a place of turmoil, instability, and stress. I applied for their U.S. immigration papers, and their petition was approved in 1983. It took another thirteen years and astronomical attorney fees to obtain their final admission to the United States. Their place of birth, Iran, was the biggest obstacle in this process. Layla's husband didn't live long enough and passed away in 2001 at the age of 84. On February 27, 2003, Layla finally received her American citizenship.

Reza became one of the most important engineers in the Iranian oil refinery in Abadan. For a number of years, he was, because of his expertise, one of very few skilled personnel who was on call at all times. As his job became more stressful and demanding, he requested a transfer to an administrative position in Tehran. After many years, and giving large sums of bribe money, known as *roshveh,* to several government officials, he was awarded one of the prestigious corporate positions at the oil company in the capital. Once there, because he had visited me in the United States and liked the life style and the freedom here, he wanted to emigrant to America; thus he applied for early retirement. I was able to obtain a business visa for him to bring his family with a permanent residency. Unfortunately, he had a more difficult time than I did in adjusting and making a better life in America. Like many other immigrants, his venture was not as successful as it could have been in his new country.

Ziba became a DJ for the Iranian national radio station where she exhibited great talent in reciting poetry accompanied by original Persian music. This was a very popular program called "*Golha.*" She also made a considerable amount of money dubbing foreign movies and TV programs into Farsi. For many years, American movies were dubbed in the native language of the country they were shown in. When I lived in Iran, I never noticed how humorous they were. However, on my last visit to Tehran, my daughters and I laughed hysterically watching Bob Hope telling his jokes in Farsi, and Robert Redford and Barbara Streisand speaking Persian in "The Way We Were."

After having four children, all one year apart, Ziba finally completed high school in Iran, which she had had to quit because of her marriage when she was in tenth grade. There was no comprehensive test, such as our GED, that Ziba could take to earn a high school diploma. The Iranian educational system required passing one grade each year, even for adults. It was amazing how she later completed her college degree at the University of Tehran while working long hours dubbing movies and taking care of children at home. She received some education in France, and earned another degree from the University of Northern Colorado in Greeley.

Ziba divorced and remarried five times. These numerous marital failures caused her heartaches and each ended in compromising situations. One of her marriages was simply to obtain a Green Card. I cherished my sister, Ziba, and her life and the way it ended almost destroyed me. In 1983, she was murdered in her home in North Carolina, having been struck in the head with an ax eleven times. I always felt that her troubled life was going to drive her to an early grave, what with her painful past, and monumental disappointments with her five husbands and four children. However, I never imagined, when I received the phone call that unforgettable day, that her life would end this way. Her killer was never found.

My father, Nader, passed away in Tehran in 1977. Ozra died in 1992.

LIFE AND HUMAN RIGHTS IN IRAN

Unlike Western civilization, which socially classifies people based on wealth as rich, middle class, and poor, Iran, during the reign of the late Shah had its own classification, a breakdown of which follows.

* The Royal Family and spouses were a class of their own.

* Below them were the upper privileged, which included prime ministers, cabinet members, government officials, heads of the military forces, secret service, etc., and their relatives. They were called The Thousand Families.

* The educated, approximately 20% of the citizens, were a significant force in the day-to-day operation of the country. This group was comprised of rich, middle class and poor. Doctors, lawyers, judges, educators, officers, and business owners were included in this group.

* The majority, approximately 65% of the population, fell into the uneducated category. Religion was their inspiration and mainstay of life. They had two separate classes among them: the poor and the barely alive. Construction workers, mechanics, blue collar professionals, carpet weavers, and alike were called poor. Labor was cheap and living expenses were very high. Four U.S. dollars per day was considered a good income for the highly skilled laborer. Long working hours were accepted part of the trade. Higher-class citizens employed their maids from this group, who worked for less than one dollar a day, plus food, housing, and clothes.

The next class, barely surviving, made me wonder how they could live under such miserable conditions. In comparison, the homeless in America would be considered middle class. Lack of water, electricity, food, sanitation, and restrooms made their life extremely unhealthy. Most Americans would not be able to tolerate such conditions for an hour. Large families lived in a dirt hole dug in the ground with a bamboo roof over it. They called some of these populated areas in the south of Tehran *Hasir Abad*, which meant the "bamboo development." While

33

the Shah featured the glamorous northern side of Tehran as part of his publicity campaign to the world, the unfortunate citizens in *Hasir Abad* lived anonymously in absolute poverty. Generally, they had large families with an average salary of less than $500 per year.

With my close friends, as part of our civic duty, I delivered bread to some in hopes of avoiding starvation. During our first visits they were so hungry they couldn't wait until we set the bread down, knocking us to the ground in their frenzy to get a piece. Bread flew everywhere, some landing on the dirt road. Even though our delivery team members were extremely strong athletes, we could not avoid getting injured by the starving villagers. One particular teammate, an exceptional wrestler, Golam Reza Takhti, who was twice the Olympic gold medalist and three times the world champion, received serious injuries a couple of times. He admitted, jokingly, that no other world wrestler had been able to knock him down as fast as the little starving youngsters did. It became impossible for us to continue our good deed. The community leaders had to assure our protection before we agreed to go back. The hunger among some was so severe that I have seen children fight over a little meat left on a bone dug from trash cans. It was meat that they did not have at home.

The goal for such desperate people was not education or any kind of future accomplishment. It was just to stay alive, to survive, each individual day! This is a life quite unimaginable for many who grow up living in Europe and America.

The Royal family lived in lavish palaces, each of which was dedicated to a special season or occasion. Those palaces were luxurious and situated in the most beautiful locations. The Shah's family also owned some of the best real estate in other countries. Those sites were for gambling, vacations, or taking a friend or mistress for a weekend of fun. Most would be vacant for years, but the family had to own and maintain them. The maids, gardeners, bodyguards, and servants were the fortunate ones living in them. It is important to mention that their water, fruit, groceries, clothes, and all other necessities were imported daily via private jets. Europe, Japan, Canada, and the U.S. were their favorite shopping grounds. Nothing produced locally was good enough for the royal family.

Knowing these conditions makes us aware that economic sanctions against poor countries is counterproductive. The only ones hurt by the sanctions are the innocent, ordinary citizens who cannot get desperately needed medicine or replacement parts for broken down equipment. Imagine surgical operations without anesthesia, broken bones set without pain killers and without casts for mending. Many people have died because something as simple as chlorine for safe drinking water fell under the sanctions. Therefore, those who truly suffer have nothing to do with the policy making. In fact, the American imposed UN sanctions have proved to be a slap in our own face. They have caused losses to many American industries by handing a perfect opportunity to other countries to make huge profits. Russia, France, Germany, Israel, China, Japan, India, and other nations have filled the void, earning billions because of U.S. imposed sanctions.

Rulers such as the late Shah of Iran, Saddam Hussein of Iraq, Milosevic of the former Yugoslavia, and the late President Deng Xiaoping of China have made alliances with any country which satisfied their personal purposes. They did not worry about concerned citizens' support or American policies. Democracy had no meaning for them. The Royal Family, their top associates, even their employees, had the power to kidnap, rape, or kill people without a legal system interfering. Often citizens' properties and businesses were taken away without legal recourse. The ones who persisted by protesting or making too many inquiries mysteriously disappeared.

Even though I hate all tyrants and dictators with a vengeance, it is important to bear in mind that they were not the ones who carried out the dirty work. It was their followers, who were as vicious as their leaders. I cannot blame the Shah or Saddam Hussein alone for the barbaric punishment carried out against their citizens. The corruption of the entire nation, particularly assistants of the royal family, heads of the government branches, staff, the secret service agents, the military officers, and even the ground soldiers who were carrying out orders were just as guilty of the crimes and should also be held accountable. It was not the rulers themselves who raped, tortured, or killed, but it was their malicious subordinates who did these heinous crimes against their own people. This specific group of people are just as evil, depraved, and corrupt as their leaders.

During Operation Desert Storm, former President George H. Bush made a statement: "Our bombing Iraq will put enough pressure on the Iraqi people to realize the need for getting rid of Saddam and replacing him." How bold, as if Mr. Bush, who previously worked for the CIA, didn't know who held the power in that country! Unless there were an American covert operation or a military coup d'etat, a change would never happen. Based on past experiences, a takeover in those countries is not necessarily for the best as the new leader or regime has often been worse. The situation in Afghanistan is a good example. Life for Afghanis has not improved after the Russian takeover, the control by the Taliban, or the American bombing in the name of fighting terrorism.

The United States' military invasion of Iraq in April 2003, as ordered by President George W. Bush, is another example of not understanding the complex issues of poverty, hunger, survival, and corruption in the Middle East. The idea of getting rid of Saddam, liberating Iraq, and creating democracy by military force is a bigger mistake than some of our past presidents' actions in that region. Democracy cannot be brought to a country by war. Real change can only happen with "education." People must be able to read and write to know their options and to vote.

Based on Leon Harris' interview (CNN, December 1996) with an American professor born in Iraq, half a million innocent Iraqi children were killed as a result of American bombing during the Gulf War. This was due to intentional or unintentional targets hit by U.S. attacks. What could their helpless parents have done to avoid such a tragedy? The most recent war against Iraq in 2003 caused even more casualties and injuries to many innocent Iraqi citizens. Uncounted lives and families have been destroyed.

Desperate, hopeless people in the Middle East have created a very favorable situation for Islamic hard-liners to take over some countries. The Imans and Mullahs want to assume the power, wealth, and authority over the people just as much as the former kings and tyrants. They are all made of the same cloth. They use Islam as a front to hide their real motives which are based on greed and not the betterment of the people. The wealth of the country would not be shared with the people or used for the improvement of its infrastructure, but rather would be stockpiled for their own personal excesses. For example, in 1982 Ayatollah Khomeini's son was apprehended in Rome with more than $250,000.00 worth of Persian rugs! The religious Imams (Islamic leaders) are supported by other fanatical leaders, such as bin Laden, which gives them more strength and followers.

Americans thought favorably of the late Shah and his great service to Iran, but it was mostly a cover-up and false publicity. Contrary to the thinking of the time, the Shah was not a great leader and took basic human rights away from the citizens. His two priorities in life were power and amassing his own personal wealth. He robbed his own people, putting on a good face to the world through skillful, controlled propaganda. With his unlimited financial power he was able to manipulate and influence American politicians, including some of our past presidents. No other leader was capable of being in bed with the Russians and the Americans at the same time. With his exceptional intelligence, he had both the White House and the Kremlin in the palm of his hand, making both sides think he was their strongest ally. In the history of modern dictators, the Shah was among the elite.

After his exile, his autobiography was aired on television where he was listed among the top dictators of the century. A British publishing company offered his second wife, Queen Soraya, ten million Pounds to write her memoir, but the Shah offered her ten times more to shut up. She wisely chose the higher and safer offer.

The combination of his enormous wealth, resources, and the country's strategic location made him a very powerful international figure. Paying hush money to the international media assured him that his public image would not be tarnished by his orders for mass executions, inhuman tortures, and mutilations. Knowing these facts and witnessing our past presidents' support of the late Shah makes me wonder about our own politicians' motives.

Many Americans think of Iran as being flat, sandy, and desert-like. Contrary to this belief, *Alborz,* Iran's highest mountain, has an elevation of 18, 940 ft. It was an ideal location for the U.S. military to install missile surveillance. There, with carte blanche approval of the Shah, they secretly observed and monitored Russian activities. This vantage point was not possible from other neighboring countries because none had the same geographical advantage. Thus, the Shah and Iran possessed a more favorable status. The Persian Gulf and oil also made Iran an important Middle Eastern nation.

The relationship between the Shah and the U.S. was tight. He had large contracts with major companies. Purchasing aircraft and helicopters and manufacturing various military goods were among his routine deals. This indirectly gave him great influence over the lobbyists and politicians on Capitol Hill.

Ironically, however, and simultaneously, Iranian Natural Gas was being piped to the Russian border. It was impossible to conceal the huge pipeline which crossed Iran from the Persian Gulf to Russia. The CIA, the U.S. military, and other responsible parties turned a blind eye. The Shah exceptionally shrewd, was the kingpin, paying everyone hush money. When people demonstrated for human rights, His Majesty's army would murder the protesters. His army would surround the helpless demonstrators with tanks and helicopters mowing them down from the air.

In one such mass-killing, which was called Black Friday, His Majesty personally led the helicopters that murdered 15,000 protesters. They were mostly women and children. With no respect for the dead and their proper burials (which is an abomination for Moslem tradition), bulldozers dumped the bodies into trucks and buried them in mass graves. This entire sordid incident was hidden from the eyes of the world. It wasn't until the overthrow of the Shah that the international news media revealed this horrendous event. How the journalists ignored that awful tragedy was another example of his ability to divert attention from his barbaric criminal acts against the citizens. No one dared to report his horrible crimes against humanity!

The news from Iran was skillfully misleading. I vividly remember a specific campaign the Shah devised, creating much publicity about his granting Iranian women the right to vote. The Americans were very impressed with this show of democracy. I must admit that he allowed the women to go to the polls, to put their ballot in the boxes the same way as the men did. But "no one" in the country had a vote that counted. The voting boxes were fixed by the Shah's men, and he always "unanimously" won. How was the world persuaded to see this as progress or to believe this to be a democracy?

Another campaign he promoted was constructing freeways in Tehran. The joke was that the only freeway built was from his palace to his hunting lodge. To add to the injustice, he did not use the freeway but rather flew by helicopter to his destinations. This not being public knowledge, the international media again had a field day with headlines boasting of His Majesty's progressive spirit. The Shah never had to deal with the horrendous traffic conditions in Tehran. When he was forced to use ground transportation, the entire route would be blocked for several hours before and after his cavalcade. Not even an emergency vehicle was permitted to cross his blockade.

The Shah had no regard for the well-being of his people. He built an opulent playground in the Persian gulf on Kiesh Island. It was better than any resort spot in the world, but it was not for citizens' use. It only served as his exclusive place of pleasure and business. This lavish resort attracted the rich oil sheiks in the region to come and spend money in his nightclubs and brothels. There they had access to the most beautiful girls and dancers who "served" the wealthy clients.

Briefly, I can best describe the Shah's powerful financial grip in the following manner: take a cab, a local flight, stay in a hotel, smoke a cigarette, watch a television show, make a phone call, buy a Mercedes sedan or a Honda motorcycle, put sugar in your tea, or any such similar activity, and in each case, some percentage of the money lands in a business controlled and owned, in whole or in part, by the Shah or his relatives. Beyond the first family, the Shah's closest friends controlled vast business empires, including monopolies and exclusive concessions conferred by the grace of the Shah. Nepotism, favoritism, and corruption have long been ubiquitous. Businesses paid licensing fees off the books. Judges were paid to settle cases. Sweetheart deals were struck between foreign investors and the royal family. Iran was one of the most corrupt countries in the world. There was no legitimate legal system - do it their way or pay the consequences.

Regardless of size, businesses in the country were forced to hang a picture of the Shah on the premises. If they did not comply, the business would be closed. Large cash penalties, torture of family members, imprisonment and temporary disappearances of attractive family members were among the customary fines for not having the royal family's picture hung in a prominent place. Meanwhile, the foreign media mis-interpreted this display of photographs and portrayed it as public admiration for the Shah.

The Shah, his family, friends, and associates transferred

large sums of money from Iran to foreign bank accounts. Swiss and American banks were among the most popular choices to hide their stolen wealth. He also owned much desirable real estate in America and gave several holdings to his associates or politicians with whom he dealt. Today there are many wealthy Iranians living in Iran and abroad who thrive on their collected fortunes. Other real estate holdings of the Shah included places in St. Moritz, Acapulco, Panama, and Egypt. It is impossible to calculate the amount of money his family and friends stole from the citizens of Iran.

Most of the world is not aware that the Iranian National Anthem had nothing to do with our history, culture, civilization, or people. It merely said, "Long live the Shah! Because of His Majesty, our land is so wonderful and prosperous!" The song continued with further praise of his Pahlavi Dynasty.

The anthem was played over and over, making most Iranians sick to their stomachs. Wherever we went, whatever we did, we had to hear it. Whether in a movie theater, watching a TV program, listening to a lecture, watching sports, or taking a class, one could not escape the lyrics. Everyone was expected to stand up, salute the Shah's image, and then go on with life. If you did not react immediately and with total respect, the SAVAK, the Shah's secret service, could arrest you on the spot. There could be many natural, little reasons for not responding quickly, an erection because of your sexy date, a sore back, your clothes caught in the chair; it did not matter. People had to jump up and stand at attention with the first note, or else.

Whether it was a minor or major offense, many individuals never made it back from his torture chambers. The Shah had his own sick way of making the punishment fit the crime. There were common consequences for public wrong doings: blinding people for reading articles against him; amputating a foot, a leg, or an arm for participating in a demonstration for freedom, even simply holding a sign had a similar punishment. This butchery

41

was performed in the SAVAK torture chambers in Evin. After the revolution, thousands of people without arms or legs paraded to exhibit the mistreatment they had suffered under the Shah. The numbers are astonishing, with more than 15,000 mutilated people participating in each parade.

The hardship many Iranians endured under the Shah's regime was terrible. One third of Iran's budget was set aside for his secret service operations. During the Nixon administration 3,000 SAVAK members had permission to operate in the U.S., intimidating thousands of American Iranians. They tortured Iranians participating in meetings or activities against His Majesty. Testimony to the SAVAK's savagery are the bodies dumped into lakes and ditches without anyone's being the wiser.

What the police got away with in Iranian police stations was a worse nightmare. Instead of protecting the public, they abused and intimated the poor, innocent citizens. Each police station had its own team of car and house thieves. They would send the thieves to burglarize homes, returning to the station with quantities of valuable goods. The stolen items were kept in huge storage rooms. Expensive Persian rugs were an extremely hot commodity. The police held the items for two to three months, waiting for the owners to buy back their own goods. If the negotiations were not satisfactory, they would be sold to others. Owners had the chance to buy their own property back, but only for a limited time. The thieves who were in cohorts with the police had to provide the police with a detailed list of which house the stolen articles belonged to, plus the date and time they were taken. This enabled the authorities to charge the proper fees. If the police needed or desired an item for themselves, they had the chance to take it.

When citizens reported a stolen item, the first question the police asked was, "How much is it worth to you?" Often a similar item from their large storage room was offered when their own stolen property was not available. It was embarrassing to buy something which may have been your neighbor's. But, unfortunately, many owners could not afford to repurchase the items in their negotiations with the police.

If prostitutes did not pay the police a generous fee and offer their services for free, they could not work the streets. Often the penalties for not being compliant were severe. Those who were not sexually desirable would be beaten and their money taken from them. Some women became indentured servants. The most attractive were gang raped and/or suffered multiple sexual abuses. The humiliations and constant abuse ensured that everyone complied. Sadly, this practice wasn't limited to hookers. It was common for the Shah's police to extend such vicious abuse to innocent members of a family and even to their close friends. Imagine being imprisoned and tortured when not having any idea what your alleged crime was!

Qualifications to obtain employment positions did not include education, experience, or skill. It was based on who you knew and how much you were willing to pay. This included how promptly the cash could be delivered to the officials in charge. It was amazing to see how many high-paying prestigious jobs were awarded to unqualified, ignorant people. Many landed these jobs because of a swinging female friend or wife who slept her husband's way to the top. If you were the only qualified person in a specific field, and that organization could not function without you, your job was secure. Otherwise, you could be replaced at any time. It is safe to say that money and sex were the tools necessary in climbing the ladder to the top.

My first wife placed a tremendous amount of pressure on me to return to Iran and take a permanent position there. Because I wanted to keep my family together, but against my own wishes, in 1974 I made a serious attempt to go back to Tehran to live. I tried my best in good faith, but realized nothing had changed for the better.

Upon arrival at Tehran's Mehr Abad airport, the government took away all Iranians' passports to maintain their control over the citizens; thus, leaving the country became almost impossible. If authorities chose not to let a person leave, the passport would not be given back. The government had an answer for everything. In our case, they said, "Your passports are with the SAVAK." Basically, it meant forget it. Without an official location or phone number for inquiries, many fools spent hours trying to find the SAVAK's office. Good luck!

I knew their game well. In hopes of getting our passports back, I had to pretend and convince a general how serious I was about taking a job,. The Shah had many generals, called *adjudans*, who were in charge of various government offices. The man with whom I was dealing was a well mannered, reputable, elderly gentleman, and fortunately a soccer fan who remembered me from my former games. He told me I was his favorite player, and recalled a few highlights from some of my best matches.

We talked at great length about my ability, qualifications, and education. However, our communication broke down when the discussion turned to what I considered my specialty. The general was adamantly concerned about my area of expertise. I reiterated each time that I had extensive knowledge of early education, believing I could establish a solid foundation in the country's Elementary Physical Education program. The general didn't want to hear it. He repeated several times that with my experience, I must only talk and concentrate on higher education, and not to waste my time with elementary school. He expressed that they needed me at the professorial level, due to the projected opening of a large University of Sports. He felt my knowledge was of much better use there than at any elementary school.

After several days of discussing salary, starting date, and their desperate need for me, I still could not come to a conclusion as to what exactly my job was going to be. He kept insisting that on my application I must include my specialty. He asked about the sports I coached in America.

Casually I replied, "Tennis, track and field, gymnastics and

44

soccer."

The general was impressed, saying, "Wow, this is what I have been asking you about several times. You are an expert in those sports. Why are you being so modest? I have never hired anyone with so many areas of expertise."

Imagine my confusion. Was I supposed to be training national athletes, university teams in those sports, or did they need me to design a curriculum for better physical education programs for all the schools in the country? I was hoping it would be the latter, because of my interest, experience, and educational strengths. I could benefit every youngster across the nation. But I did not think the general even slightly had that in mind.

On the last day of our meetings, he suddenly offered me a once-in-a-lifetime position. The general said he had been speaking to His Majesty the night before and was pleased to appoint me to the position of Head Coach/Manager of the Prince Reza Pahlavi. My job was to ensure that the Majesty's son received the best coaching available anywhere in the world. If I couldn't find the best coach in a sport, then it was my responsibility to train him. He mentioned an open budget for hiring the coaches, and my salary would be three times more than what he offered for teaching at the university.

I knew that we were in the last quarter of this political game. I had my chance to score the winning point against him; therefore, I showed enormous excitement for the position by hugging and kissing him on both cheeks. I needed our passports to leave and this demonstration was the way to ensure it. The deal was set. All that remained was my returning to the States and tying up loose ends before I could return to Iran. The general was under the impression that this would only take a week or two. It ended up lasting the rest of my life.

After our lengthy handshake he made a phone call. Within an hour our passports and necessary papers were to be delivered to me at his office. All I had to do was play it cool until I could get myself and my family out of the country.

Now, here comes the twist. Everything was progressing according to my plans. There seemed to be no problem in the process, except one small misinterpretation. I was lost when the general wanted to know my plans about taking care of the "ironing fee." His statements regarding his wish for removal of wrinkles totally confused me. I could not understand what he wanted me to say or do. He repeated three times: "With a little ironing, we will smooth out the wrinkles and everybody will be happy. It won't be much, say, 70,000 tomans ($10,000 U.S. dollars in 1974)." I was totally confused. None of his words made sense to me. What money? What ironing fee? What wrinkles and what did $10,000 have to do with my new job offer?

Apparently, living in the United States, focusing on my education at graduate school, I had forgotten the corrupt Iranian system for getting ahead. There *roshveh*, bribe, was the real means for any advancement, not simple honest work. The general, frustrated by my ignorance, exhausted himself trying to make me understand what he meant. He lost his calm, stating angrily, "Money, stupid, money is what it takes to finalize this deal!" He went on to scream, "What the hell did they teach you in America? They gave you a doctoral degree, a lousy piece of paper? You are still dumber than our elementary school kids in common business sense. How do you think our system works here? Do you expect a job like this grows on trees? In your little brain, perhaps no one deserves to benefit from creating a dream position such as the one I made up for you!" As I sat there silently, he continued with alarming frustration, "People need to harvest the fruit of their hard work."

By then I realized what was expected. I was not going to let my victory slip away at the finish line. Skillfully I apologized, placing all the blame on American education. Playing dumb, I told the general that America was at fault for not having taught me life in the real world. In order to salvage my plans, I made sure he believed there would be no problem in taking care of his "wrinkles." To regain his trust, I innocently asked him if he wouldn't mind taking the "ironing fee" in two payments. The first upon my return from America, the second with my first paycheck. This appeased him enough to ring for tea in celebration.

While we were having our tea a young police officer knocked, entered his office, and handed our passports to him. Shaking hands the general gave me the documents, wishing me good luck, a safe trip and speedy return. Still playing their game, I thanked him profusely and asked him to give me a list of whatever he wanted from America. First, he said no thanks, just your quick return is my present. Knowing their custom, I asked again. After the third time he reached into his pocket and handed me a long list with 32 items. I was supposed to bring him nine pairs of Levi jeans, in different sizes and lengths, several bottles of expensive whisky, a variety of perfumes, and more. With extreme joy, which I am sure he interpreted in the wrong way, with a pretense of being grateful I exited his office.

Once outside the building I jumped into my rental car, driving home like a bat out of hell. I made the plane reservations and we flew out the next day. Although nervous and scared, I took off hoping that if I ever went back, it would not be to the same corruption. Later, I added up the monetary value on his wanted list; it exceeded $1,800!

On the flight from Tehran to London, I couldn't stop crying for the rest of the nation. Thinking about the citizens who had to deal with the day-to-day corruption and absence of human rights made my heart ache. Many sad memories flashed through my mind as the plane sped from my homeland. As nervous as I was, I quietly thanked "Allah" for helping me get as far away from there as I could.

Although I was out of Iran, flying toward freedom, my thoughts were on the Shah's last words to me in obtaining his permission to come to America in 1967, "Don't ever think that you are not coming back." He would not allow any of his educated, talented people to leave Iran permanently. I was young, energetic, creative, a former top athlete, and then a

47

successful coach. It made me a prime candidate to be on his Most Wanted List. He once asked me, "Why do you want to go to America?" I replied, "For my graduate degree." Casually he mentioned that it wasn't necessary for me to go. All I needed to do was tell him from which university I wanted my degree. He would obtain the desired diploma for me, without my leaving the country.

I am sure this is hard for Americans to understand. He was so rich and powerful that anything he wanted could be bought for the right price. If any university needed funds, the Shah without hesitation would donate a check for over $25 million. These kinds of small financial transactions, though enormous to most, would be considered a drop in the bucket to him. In return, they would give him whatever he asked without questions.

When I refused to accept such a diploma he was impressed, responding, "That's what I like about you, Parviz. Unlike most of these parasites around me, you have always earned your accomplishments. Just remember, don't think for a second that you are not coming back."

Even with such fear instilled in my mind, I never thought it would be easy to stay away permanently. Yet, I was ready and determined to give my best shot and start a new life in America no matter what.

All these thoughts raced through my mind during our flight to London. They incited memories of life under the Shah. Once, when our team was competing in Italy, three of my teammates convinced our coach to give them their passports. Normally the coach or the head delegate held the passports in his possession, treating us like a military unit. Furthermore, with each team they sent enough SAVAK members to monitor every move. Three players came up with brilliant excuses and got their passports from the coach for a few minutes. Unbeknownst to the rest of the team one remained in Italy, the other two escaped to Germany. Luckily, they had girlfriends who hid them for almost a year. These defections outraged the Shah as his best players, consistently scoring in games against other national teams, were not playing for him. He wanted them back but I thought their biggest crime must have been beating the Shah's system. There is no need to write about what became of the coach and his career after this unforgivable mistake. The SAVAK arrested and tortured the families of the runaway athletes until they eventually returned to Iran.

The Shah employed experienced CIA experts from the Vietnam War, who had tortured the Viet Cong, to train the SAVAK at Evin Prison. They implemented methods such as breaking bones, hanging victims in very painful positions, along with other barbaric torture techniques to force them to talk. If that did not work, they would hack off an arm or leg of a child, a sister or brother until they were given the information they wanted.

Without established laws for human rights, there was no way to prove these tortures, let alone stop them. I was struck with the recurring vision of a morning when the entire neighborhood gathered around the smashed body of my neighbor, Hussein, a 59-year-old, well-respected man. His 32-year-old son was part of the underground revolution against the Shah. A team of seven SAVAK members went to his house in search of the son or information leading to his whereabouts. The poor man did not know how to reach his son, as the latter was an adult and no longer lived at home. Not believing him, they proceeded to tie him up, undressing his wife and four daughters. They brutally gang-raped them one at a time in front of Hussein and the grandchildren to force him to disclose his son's address. The information, he honestly did not have.

The victims ranged in age from fourteen to fifty. According to their cultural beliefs, no other man but the husband or father was allowed to see his wife or daughters without the *chador*, in public. The next day that decent gentleman, unable to deal with his shame, threw himself from the fifth floor of a building. He just could not live, humiliated and disgraced in front of his family for not being able to protect them.

49

Even today I have a difficult time understanding how the world allowed the Shah to maintain his evil regime. President Carter's motto was "Human Rights;" yet, he supported the Shah, culminating in the hostage crisis of 1979. I presume Mr. Carter meant human rights for select nations, not for others.

During the last years of the Shah's reign, the U.S. ambassador to Iran was Richard Helms. Before this appointment Helms was the director of the CIA. American politicians and presidents backed the Shah, under the pretext that such support was necessary to stop communism. Communism was nothing compared to the dictatorship of the Shah. He was in the same league as Milosevic, Adolph Hitler, and Saddam Hussein; nothing stopped him from pursuing his cruel criminal activities. The entire nation was held hostage, with every citizen being his victim.

Iranians felt it was impossible to remove the Shah from power. Much to everyone's surprise, a man named Ayatollah Khomeini, a very powerful religious leader, was the one person in the world who could overthrow him. Before Khomeini was exiled to France in 1962 he had influence over 80 percent of the citizens. For Shi'a Moslems he was the equivalent of the Pope to Catholics. The masses flocked to hear his words. This, of course, made the Shah quite nervous. He was not going to let any religious or political leader usurp his hold over the nation. The Shah, who generally had no problem eliminating anyone, was terrified to kill Khomeini because of his tremendous influence over the people. Instead he forced Khomeini into exile that lasted seventeen years.

In 1979 Khomeini returned to Iran. At that time the remaining 20% of the population, who were not religious but could no longer tolerate the Shah, turned to him. With the entire country out of desperation supporting him, Khomeini was able to oust the Shah. Upon announcing his return to Iran, he asked the military to put down their weapons and surrender. They complied, thus avoiding the inevitable bloodshed which usually follows an overthrow of a regime. The Iranians poured into the streets, rejoicing over his homecoming. All who previously were against the Shah combined their forces and supported the Ayatollah.

The Shah seeing the power this man had over the masses fled the country in fear. Unfortunately, the killings resumed after the revolution. This time, however, the ones being executed were the men who had kept the Shah in power. His generals, political leaders, and associates posed the threat of a coup d'etat, and they had to be eliminated in order to keep the Shah from regaining his power.

Ayatollah Khomeini was well aware of Iran's history. When Prime Minister Dr. Mohammed Mossaddegh, the country's only hope for freedom and democracy, didn't execute his enemies, he did not live long enough to see his dreams for a free Iran come true.

Dr. Mossaddegh had received his doctoral degree in law from the University of The Hague, the Netherlands. He served as prime minister believing that as with any monarchy, the Shah was only a figurehead and that the parliament and prime minister were the legal governing body. The Shah's duties and functions were merely a formality. That did not go well with the Shah. He didn't care what the law was.

Among Dr. Mossaddegh's several accomplishments was nationalizing Iran's oil. For many years the British had been taking Iranian oil for free. Returning the ownership to Iran was a huge economic boon to the country. Possessing a brilliant legal mind, he was intent on making Iran a free, independent nation. Well versed in constitutional rights, Mossaddegh made human rights his main goal for the people, thus garnering a tremendous following and gaining much popularity.

The Shah with all his military might knew the power of the people. For his protection and a possible quick escape he had a runway built behind his palace for his 747 jet plane. His pilots were ready to take off instantly. Nicknamed "the suitcase monarch," the Shah could leave at a moments notice.

Fearing for his life with the emergence of Dr. Mossaddegh's

followers, he fled the country in 1953. Regrettably, America labeled Dr. Mossadegh a communist and, instead of helping him and the Iranian people in their quest for freedom, instigated a military coup restoring the Shah to power.

The irony was that during Mossaddegh's brief attempt at reforming Iran, his cabinet members, advisors, and staff told him to be wary of the Shah's men. They knew that they were diligently planning to bring the Shah back. They advised Mossaddegh to either assassinate those people or incarcerate them. Predating Martin Luther King, Dr. Mossaddegh insisted on nonviolent resistance. He was a supreme human being, believing that murder was inhuman. He wished to establish a truly democratic nation.

In 1979, twenty-six years later, the Ayatollah Khomeini was not about to make the same mistake. Knowing that the Shah's people could not be trusted, he executed anyone who posed a threat to his newly established leadership. Because Khomeini was able to overthrow the Shah easily, the Iranians began to regard him as more than human. As the leader of the new Islamic Republic Government, Khomeini was regarded by Iranians as either God or his messenger, *Imam*. This spurred a frenzy of religious worship. The United States was caught off guard by his sudden and dramatic takeover. Americans had no time to shut down their military bases. Losing billions of dollars in military equipment, all personnel were evacuated leaving everything behind.

At present, Iran is rife with problems. Thrown back to the Dark Ages by the Islamic Republic and strapped by a very poor economy, the country is bankrupt. Power outages, water shortages, and food lines are daily occurrences. Lack of education, medication, and most necessities of life has created undesirable living conditions.

More than seventy per cent of the citizens of Iran are under the age of 25 and know no other life than living under the restrictive Islamic government. Educated citizens, college students, journalists, and writers are trying to make a difference and demonstrations against the government are routine occurrences. Unfortunately, the heavy-handed Mullahs have imprisoned, executed, and tortured many of these people. A professor from the University of Tehran was executed in December 2002 for saying in his class "We don't all have to act like monkeys in following the Koran, specifically with the Mullahs' interpretation."

However, a few signs of cultural change can be seen in public places and educational institutions in Iran. While the older women wear the traditional black chador, many of the younger women can be seen in colorful head scarves with some hair showing and long coats. Many women express their individualism by accessorizing with designer purses and sunglasses. They have the right to vote and many are employed in the parliament and government positions. Change will come slowly to the Middle East. Iran is no exception, but Iranians are looking to and hoping for a brighter future.

It is a miracle that for the first time in history, in May, 1997 Iranians had the right to choose their president. I congratulate them with the highest admiration from the bottom of my heart and wish the citizens the best of luck and happiness in their "New Life - New Country." With electing an educated, moderate president, as is Mr. Khatami, I pray that life for Iranians now will bring the kind of bright future that they deserve. I hope our American presidents will extend a hand of friendship to establish diplomacy and economic trade between the two nations. This definitely would be the right step in establishing the free democratic society that Iranians deserve. President Khatami's January 7, 1998 interview with Christiane Amanpour on CNN, entitled "Iran-A New Beginning," offered the most promising news to realize how ready and willing Iran is to put the past behind and start a new, healthy diplomatic relationship with the United States. What happened in the past is history and nothing can change it.

Lately, U.S. politicians along with the media blame Iran for supporting Islamic fundamentalists for some of the recent terrorist acts. *Mojahedin* is an Arabic word meaning fighters. *Hezboallah* is another word meaning "Allah's Union." They are religious fanatics the same as are some so-called Christians who burned abortion clinics in America. I find it very hard to believe that Iran, with a 40 percent inflation rate, is the only country supporting these terrorists, but listening to the news one is led to believe that it may be the case. Both countries must move forward.

Additional external factors that have made Iranian life more miserable are: 1) being labeled as part of the Axis of Evil, 2) the fear that the Taliban and Al-Qaeda who have fled Afghanistan are hiding in Iran, 3) refugees from Iraq, 4) being accused of having nuclear capabilities, and 5) being accused of harboring terrorists. All these facts open the possibility that Iran would be the next country with which America would be going to war. The combination of the above problems without a hopeful future makes life for Iranians stressful and worrisome.

The successful take over of Islamic Government by Ayatollah Khomeini has created a copycat situation for the rest of the Islamic hard-liners in the region. It also has given the Al-Qaeda a good reason to seek the same in some key countries in the Middle East, especially Egypt, Saudi Arabia, and very possibly Iraq.

Little is known of the fact that in the mid 80's, there were two hundred thousand Iranians detained in Turkey, living in tents under sad quarantine conditions. It was as heartbreaking as the situation involving refugees from Kosovo and Afghanistan. No country gave them refugee status because they were labeled "terrorists." Many of these unfortunate people were talented and highly educated, ranging from surgeons to college professors, judges, lawyers, and so on. They could not go back to Iran, either because living under strict Islamic rules was impossible for them or they held high positions during the Shah's reign and were on the most-wanted list. The only hope or assistance they received, aside from that of the Turkish government, was donations from Iranians around the world who sent food and clothing.

With the dissolution of the Shah's control, no Iranian citizen has to deal with their wives, daughters and loved ones being kidnapped, raped, or dumped into a lake. His family, workers, and secret police cannot intimidate the nation as they did for years. Nonetheless, corruption and favoritism still exists in the system. Human rights are still ignored. Some things are better than before, and other things are worse. Conditions have improved for the poor, but the educated middle and upper class are the ones now in Iran who are hurting the most.

Unfortunately, some things may never change, as SAVAK now is called *SAMAVAK,* meaning "Counter Information." Bribes have always been a part of the culture, but now they are even more common and accepted. The officials consider this "tip money" and expect people to pay automatically. Alcohol is forbidden in Islam; however, there is always the Black Market, and the business is booming. One can find any kind of liquor as long as one can pay the price!

It is unfair to call all Middle Easterners or Moslems terrorists. Those who fled their debased country in search of a better, free life are decent, intelligent, and very likable human beings. I admire in particular the late Governor Lawton Chiles of Florida for his acknowledgment and appreciation of Iranian Americans with his designation of March 21, 1997 as Iranian Heritage Day in Florida. This was the first time since the hostage crisis that an American politician has expressed a favorable statement about Iranians in America. A copy of his declaration follows at the end of this chapter. I would like to applaud governor Chiles for this dedication. Later a few others, including President Clinton followed him in recognizing the valuable services that Iranians in America have contributed to our country .

On the other hand, I can't begin to express my true feelings about the shameful behavior of the U.S. consul in Frankfurt, Germany who denied a temporary visa for my niece in February, 1997. She desperately needed a visa to visit her dying father who was undergoing a liver cancer operation at Baptist Hospital in Miami. At the same time, her older brother was scheduled to have a cancerous tumor removed from his spine. Her relatives in Germany, who owned an established business in Dusseldorf, offered the consul any kind of warranty, bond, or collateral as guarantee for her prompt return from America. In addition, her younger brother in America guaranteed her timely departure from the United States. All these guarantees were to no avail. The consul instead spitefully put an official rejection stamp on her passport, prohibiting a visitor's visa to the United States for the next two years.

I recall my most painful experience in seeking employment in 1980. Even though I was an American citizen, based on disclosure of my birth place on the application or my Middle Eastern name in the initial inquiry, I was unable to obtain any kind of position.

I had exceptional recommendations and an impressive resume that made it difficult to ignore my qualifications. However, none of my capabilities assisted me in getting a desperately needed job. This may be hard to believe, but honestly, I applied to sixty-eight institutions and corporations including used car and furniture salesmanship, rental management, and whatever help wanted ads I could find, in addition to teaching and educational vacancies, with no luck.

The sixty-ninth organization was Red Sandstone Elementary School in Eagle County, Colorado. Gary Denker, principal at the time, was a wonderful person who disregarded my place of birth and hired me based on my personal qualifications. During my employment in Eagle County I received numerous honors and awards, including: Profile of Dedication and Inspiration - Eagle County School District 1983-1984; recognition for excellence and outstanding leadership by the Board of Education, January 13, 1993; Outstanding Teacher Award, Eagle County School District, May 1995. For six years (1988-1994) my school, Red Sandstone Elementary was Colorado State Champion, for having the most physically fit students in the state because of my teaching method and my inspiring students to reach their best, and "going for the gold."

America's inconsistent policies regarding Iran and its treatment of Iranians raises a serious question about what happened to our humanity and real American compassion for mankind. Our great nation has been built on immigrants. Now, it looks like our government policies are based on who can pay what quantity to influential politicians in order to pass any kind of favorable laws from which benefits can be gained.

For decades Russians were thought of as our number-one enemies. These days they are considered our friends. We grant them immigrant status without a problem. Businesses import workers from the former USSR; Summit County in Colorado has a number of Russian employees at their stores. Surprisingly, some are entitled to $5,000 in federal funds as start up money while visas are granted automatically. In contrast, I applied for American citizenship for my older sister in 1983. It took twenty years before she received her naturalization papers.

It is an unfair and biased policy which big business and corporations have persuaded our politicians to pass. The Russian mafia in our country is the most dangerous group to fear. Many American citizens have suffered from their actions. President Carter exhibited great generosity toward Cuban prisoners and criminals under his motto of human rights and had U.S. immigration agents in Miami waiting on the shore to issue their visas as the criminals walked off the ships. Fidel Castro had a field day releasing them from his crowded jails!

During the hostage crisis in Iran I was emotionally torn. I had a very difficult time dealing with it because I could see both sides, both negatively and positively.

As a U.S. citizen I hated the hostage takers for holding 52 of my fellow Americans against their wishes for the purpose of making a point. At the same time, I knew how strongly the Iranian citizens felt. All they had asked of President Carter was not to allow their former tyrant dictator, the Shah, into the United States. They hated him for leaving Iran bankrupt by taking the country's money. Even though he was arguably the wealthiest man in the world, out of spite he made sure that the nation would suffer financially for ousting him.

I am quite patriotic and proud of my American citizenship. It upsets me terribly when anyone shows hatred toward my new country. The slogans "Death to America" or "The Great White Satan" in their rallies hurt me enormously. However, knowing why they were doing it made life very difficult for me as an American during that period. Receiving strange phone calls and having rocks thrown through my living room window in the middle of the night were not pleasant experiences. But a close honest look at our inconsistent dealings with Iran in the last several decades makes it hard to blame those demonstrators.

President Carter's actions and policies toward Iran were something else. I was relieved to see that his rescue mission failed in the preliminary stage, otherwise, not a single hostage would have been alive to rescue. His subsequent decisions, however, caused many innocent deaths and imprisonment. When Iranians in the U.S. protested against America by burning the U.S. flag, President Carter ordered all illegal Iranians to be deported immediately.

This order was illogical. People living illegally in a country wouldn't dare to bring attention to themselves in front of international news cameras. The ones burning the flags were students with legal visas protesting what they viewed as an injustice. Iranians living illegally here remained low-key and stayed out of the public eye. But it was these people who were arrested and sent back to Iran. Sadly, when they returned, they commonly were tortured and executed. Khomeini and his associates were suspicious of everyone. It was a critical time for them trying to hold on to their control. The Iranian officials incorrectly labeled the poor returning citizens deported from the U.S. as part of a CIA spy ring, assigned to overthrow the new government.

During the Shah's reign, rich American businessmen had catered to the Shah because he was "Big Money" and they loved the smell of his wealth and opulence. Every mechanical part in Iran, from F-16 bombers to tractors, lawn mowers, electric shavers, and calculators were American-made and purchased from the United States.

The country's survival, after the Shah's reign still required America-made parts, a fact already quite evident during the long eight-year war with Iraq. Replacement parts were needed for every military machine, especially the fighter bombers.

The irony of the situation surfaces once again as Khomeini approached Israel as the middle man in purchasing the needed parts from the United States. The shipments were sent to Iran via Switzerland.

Meanwhile, as Russia, China, Germany, Japan, and Switzerland extended their support to the new regime, America continued to undermine it. Both President Reagan and President Bush misjudged the power of Khomeini and thought that Saddam Hussein could easily take over Iran. They gave their allegiance to him and supported Hussein with loans.

President Reagan and the Iran-Contra Affair proved to be another incident which caused mistrust for the U.S. The President sent Oliver North as his messenger to Iran. North carried a letter and a Bible to Khomeini as a sign of good faith to establish a new, meaningful relationship between the two countries. Mr. Reagan offered Iran the badly needed shipment of parts. Knowing Iran's desperation, North delivered planeloads of equipment and parts to Iran, but behind the scenes, America supported Saddam's overthrow of Khomeini. They sold the materials to Iran at inflated prices and sent the money to Nicaragua to support the Contras in their struggle against the Sandinistas. When the truth surfaced about the scandalous deal, President Reagan at first denied it. Then he admitted his knowledge of a "small" shipment, but without accepting any personal responsibility. This again categorized

America, in the eyes of the Iranians, as a country not to be trusted.

Instead of admitting the truth, Col. North in his defense at the Iran-Contra hearings proudly justified his actions and his position by expressing, "We were stopping communism in Nicaragua with the Ayatollah's money, not the American taxpayers'."

The hearing committee did not penalize him. Some even applauded him and praised his loyalty. From the Iranian's point of view, that was another failure in establishing a trusting relationship between the two countries. Col. North was seen as a crooked ambassador of American policy. That money wasn't Khomeini's; it belonged to the starving citizens. They were the ones dying from hunger, lack of basic necessities, and medicine.

Making matters worse, President Bush provided Saddam Hussein with detailed maps of Iran's strategic bases so that they could be destroyed. All modern secret war weapons had been purchased from America by the late Shah, and American companies had built proper locations and facilities to hide them. It was a stab in the back for Iran for the U.S. to assist Saddam, their enemy, and even an enemy of America's interests. Iranians believed that Iran had paid for those weapons and had helped the American economy in the process.

Khomeini won the war despite the disadvantages. The victory, however, was very costly. Thousands of young boys between the ages of ten and fourteen were slaughtered. The Ayatollah promised their parents "the Key to Heaven" for sending their children to fight against the Iraqis. These innocent children walked in front of the soldiers to discharge the mines, so that the army could safely advance behind them. Many children were blown to bits. Winning the war against Iraq was essential for survival and Khomeini believed this was the only way to achieve it.

Now, after all that has happened, I pray that our presidents will change the traditional policy of hatred for Iran and seek new avenues of mutual respect and support. Being honest and truthful is the best way of showing the real American spirit and sense of humanity. I am sure it will take time. Iranians are ready and, according to Mr. Khatami, are changing their attitudes. It is time for the American government to extend a sincere helping hand toward them. It wouldn't be difficult if we only could change our thinking about the outcome of the hostage crisis, something which happened more than twenty years ago. It is part of history and we all must move on. Life must go forward. We must learn from our past mistakes to avoid repeating them. The slaughter of the Jews by the Nazis, dropping the atom bomb on Hiroshima, the Vietnam War, and other horrible incidents, as deplorable as they were, happened in the past. Even though we cannot forget, we must forgive in an effort to grow together and live peacefully in our global world.

IRANIAN HERITAGE DAY

WHEREAS, on March 21, 1997, people of Iranian heritage throughout the world will celebrate the first day of spring and the arrival of the Iranian New Year 1376; and

WHEREAS, Iranian Americans have contributed richly to Florida's social mosaic and to its dynamic economic growth; and

WHEREAS, individuals of Iranian heritage have earned an esteemed place in the cultural, economic and social structure of the state of Florida and have proved themselves an asset to the community with many of them holding positions in the fields of medicine, research, education, law, business, the arts and public services; and

WHEREAS, we salute Iran's historic achievement, support her search for freedom and peace and join her in celebration of this special time of year;

NOW, THEREFORE, I, Lawton Chiles, Governor of the state of Florida, do hereby designate March 21, 1997, as *IRANIAN HERITAGE DAY* in recognition of the contributions of the Iranian Community to our state, and send best wishes for a most enjoyable celebration with continued mutual understanding and friendship between our native residents and our residents of Iranian descent.

IN WITNESS WHEREOF, I have hereunto set my hand and caused the Great Seal of the state of Florida to be affixed at Tallahassee, the Capital, this 28th day of October in the year of our Lord nineteen hundred and ninety-six.

GOVERNOR

CULTURAL DIFFERENCES

Our world is made up of many people with many different beliefs, ideas, viewpoints, and dreams. Unique and beautiful traditions are ceremoniously and lovingly passed on from one generation to the next with great honor and reverence.

Imagine if we all were the same: one race, one color, one physical shape, one language, and one way of behaving. How dull our world would be! We are not identical, and it is our differences which make each one of us and our countries fascinating. How exciting it is to learn about other nationalities, to study other cultures, and to travel and explore the world in its entirety.

Having said this, it is all well and good for the armchair traveler or adventurous tourist, but for those who emigrate to a new country, it is a different story. They are often torn between leaving their old and familiar traditions and accepting and assimilating to a new or unfamiliar lifestyle, beliefs, ideas, and viewpoints.

Let us examine, for instance, the status of the male in Asian societies. In the family, generally the man is the head of the household and the primary financial provider. This tradition carries on into their governmental setup and in business, where men normally hold the senior positions. Their role, their traditions, and their values are not open for negotiation or debate. Thus, one can see that Middle Eastern views held by the typical Asian male are closely tied to their old cultural traditions.

The status of women in Asia is probably the issue most Americans are familiar with and the profound single difference between Western and Eastern civilizations. In Asian cultures, unless a woman is extremely exceptional, she normally will not be nominated to a position of authority as she is considered to be the nurturer and caretaker of the family.

The person we are has as much to do with the culture, traditions, morals, religion, and language we were taught as children as it does with our choice of lifestyle. Simply stated, we are a product of our parents' upbringing and the country in which we were born. For example, a native American Indian born and raised on a reservation typically will follow the lifestyle of his forefathers.

If we were to take identical twins at birth and place them in two separate families, one in Ireland and the other in China, they would become two different adults. Their lives would be a reflection of the specific geographical location and culture where they were raised. One would be influenced by Western culture based on the "Fight and Win" philosophy, and the other would believe in an Eastern culture which embodies the "Give and Accept" philosophy. They may be identical in looks and personality because of the same genes or possess the same qualities and talents, as both being painters, athletes, musicians, and so on. But their lives would be entirely different based on their cultural upbringing and religion. One may become a member of the IRA, maiming and killing Protestants, while his identical twin is a peaceful fisherman living with a family in a small village praying to Buddha.

Because I was born in Iran, I am a Moslem. If Israel, Greece, Tibet, or the United States were my places of birth, I probably would be a Jew, a Greek Orthodox, a Buddhist, or a Christian.

Sadly and ironically religion is still the main conflictive issue on so many levels with so many people. Personally, I believe all religions have the same goals. The outward appearances may be different but the message or wisdom is the same. Whether we worship in a synagogue, mosque, church, or temple, in my opinion, we all are going to the same station, only on different trains.

Many immigrants, myself included, do not want to convert to a new religion. But the complicated part for us is trying to integrate our religious and traditional beliefs into a Western culture which is so dramatically liberal compared to our conservative one.

For example, in my old country, the role of parents is of utmost importance. Parental respect is one of the most valued traits in Middle Eastern culture and tradition. Unlike in America, where children cannot wait to become eighteen years old to be independent of their parents, there is no emancipation age in most Asian cultures. Parents are deeply involved in choosing a lifetime partner for their youngsters. Sons or daughters, even at the age of fifty, normally do not smoke, quarrel, or slouch with their legs on top of the table while talking with their parents. They may be more educated than the parents, but on important issues courtesy will still be shown in seeking the advice of their father before making an important decision. Such courtesy is a sign of respect for the many parental sacrifices made in raising them. Children thus commonly seek parental advice until their death. This does not mean that they are not able to make decisions of their own, but it is a part of the culture and tradition to place the parents in an honorary position. Quite naturally, when youngsters show respect to their parents, they receive much more in return.

On the other hand, it seems not unusual in America for children to have to be asked twice to do just about anything. Often, something as simple as taking a daily shower turns into a major argument. Typically, surviving our children's teenage years makes us prematurely gray! Immigrants with whom I visited whose children had become Americanized had a frustrating and heartbreaking time.

The following paragraph, taken from The Lonely Planet-China, 5th edition, 1996 although addressing Chinese culture, is also applicable to many Islamic countries.

"Patterns of obedience are inextricably bound up in Chinese society. Women obey and defer to men, younger brothers to elder brothers and sons to fathers. Respect flows upwards, from young to old, from subject to ruler. Age is venerated since it gives everything (including people, objects and institutions) their dignity and worth; the elderly may be at their weakest physically, but they are at the peak of their wisdom. The family retains its central place as the basic unit of society. The key to family order is filial piety, children's respect for and duty towards their parents. There are strict codes of obedience, as well as the concept of 'face'- which can be loosely described as "status", "ego" or "self respect." Essentially, "saving face" is about avoiding being made to look stupid or being forced to back down in front of others."

Keeping this in mind, it is easy to understand the pain, embarrassment, and humiliation the immigrant parent endures when their children are unruly and defiant.

Having a "girlfriend" or a "boyfriend" is unheard of and spending time alone on a date is even worse! So, when a daughter sashays through the front door with her new male companion who is sporting a pony tail, earrings not only through his ears but nose, lip, and belly button, with pants barely hanging onto his waist and dragging the ground, you can well imagine the dismay not only on the parents' faces but in their hearts.

In Iran parents guide and help children in marriage, which does not necessarily mean forcing them to marry without consideration of love. Such guidance provides a more stable family life with a much smaller percentage of divorces and eliminates the need for costly therapy for misbehaved children. Because families stay together, school drop outs, drug related incidents, and social diseases so typical of the twenty-first century are practically nonexistent.

Occasionally, there are parents who misuse their authority and force their children to marry the wrong person; but they would be among the small minority. My father was one. He did injustice to us in every aspect of our lives. Forcing my sister, Ziba, to marry an older man was a typical, insensitive, and wrongful act on his part. It was a personal decision and had nothing to do with the beliefs and behavior of the majority of Iranians. Actually Nader did not believe in any religion. Perhaps, if he had been a good Moslem, he would have been a better human being.

Parents, being wiser, are expected to be better judges of character in selecting a life mate for their loved ones. In addition, without emotional involvement, they can choose a more suitable partner than an immature and emotionally excited teenager. It seems so obvious and simple. Their choices are based on logic rather than blind love. Criteria established for selecting a mate in Moslem tradition are based on common sense. First, financial stability for the newlyweds is the most important factor. A gorgeous hunk who has no money, education, or a dependable job would be great to go to bed with but would not guarantee shelter, shoes, clothes, or schooling for the family. Parental involvement assures that the children and the grandchildren have a place to live and food to eat and that the basic necessities are provided to avoid hardship.

Second, stability and dependability are highly sought qualities in a future wife/husband. With this in mind, they evaluate the education, intelligence, skills, and personality as indications for whether a spouse would be capable or not of taking care of a family. A man must be able to provide the financial necessities, including a promising future for his children. In a woman, they expect that she should be able to demonstrate family management, organization, and togetherness all of which are definitely needed to create a successful home environment.

Third, character and personality are additional factors to analyze. Parents would like to know if the future husband is a thoughtful person or a careless individual or a playboy. Is the future wife a loose woman who enjoys sleeping around for fun or is she a good role model as a mother for the children? Can she provide a happy home for the family?

Considering all the above factors, it should not be too difficult to realize that Moslem parents are helpful family resources and not antagonists, the way most Westerners perceive them. Nothing is wrong with parents having a significant role in evaluating a lifetime partner. They can provide better choices for their young, inexperienced son or daughter who is blinded by love. It could prevent future failure and assure a more stable life. Frankly, when we fall in love, especially at an early age, our emotions strongly effect our ability to make a sound decision. An old Persian saying is, "We need two lives on this planet, one to learn in, the other, to use our past experiences." Iranian children wisely use their parents' experiences and guidance for success.

Even in extreme cases of poverty, when a father is forced to conquer his pride and give up his son or daughter to a wealthy family as a servant, it is with the hope and understanding that his child will have a better place to live, food to eat, and clothes to wear. What happens to the child's future or how badly they may be abused depends on the decency of the wealthy family with whom they live. This is no different than putting a child up for adoption in any country. The aim is to provide a better home, but what happens to them or what their future may hold is very difficult to predict.

In a worse case scenario, poverty in Nepal provided an unfortunate opportunity for professional dealers to earn a great deal of money from the sale of children living in hopeless circumstances. Dealers skillfully convinced the parents that they were representing wealthy families who needed young female servants. They offered a sizable down payment to the fathers, and assured them that their daughters, living with rich families, would have food, clothing, a comfortable place to sleep, plus a good monthly salary. The amount of money paid was based on age and beauty, with virgins valued even more. Offers were hard to refuse because parents couldn't financially support their children.

After the parents signed the agreement, the dealers took the innocent girls to Bombay, India, and sold them into prostitution for the over 200,000 men living in the city. They were beaten and tortured if they didn't comply fully. These young girls ranged anywhere from nine to fourteen years old. Sex-related communicable diseases became an integral part of their lives and sixty percent of working girls were tested HIV positive. They had to work at least ten days per month to pay the madame. Other expenses required additional days and even water had to be purchased from the madame. The girls were locked in rooms until they complied and were never allowed to go into the streets. Rape, sodomy, physical and verbal abuse filled their new lives.

Disregarding such exceptions, Asian parents in general sacrifice everything for their children.

Marriage has a different value in every culture. For instance, in most Islamic countries, the bride's financial security is the main objective. It is considered a successful marriage if the wife never has to work or worry about finances during her lifetime. Primary duties for women include being a good cook, home maker, and full-time mother. Husbands are responsible for providing a comfortable home and a stable financial resource for the family.

Divorce is not nearly as common in Eastern cultures as it is in Western countries. It might have to do with the fact that most of the family laws are written to benefit men. By law, the father has custody of the children in a divorce. If he does not want them, then they are given to the mother. In most cases, the father keeps the children; thus a mother thinks twice before asking for a divorce because she loves her children so much and cannot bear to be away from them.

A traditional Persian wedding is elaborate, religious, lengthy, and expensive. Social status, education, religion, and the financial capability of the groom could alter some of the requirements; however, most customs cannot be changed. The groom or his family are responsible for the entire expenses in a wedding.

Purchases paid for by the groom in a Persian wedding are the first major hurdle to cross. They include the bridal gown, often more than one, if two or more ceremonies are performed, bridesmaids' dresses, new clothes for female family members, several wedding rings, precious gifts of jewelry, a silver or gold framed mirror, gold coins, a crystal bowl with gold fish, rice sugar candies, and silver candelabras. Another requirement is a *Koran*, the Moslem holy book, which could cost anywhere from $10.00 to $10,000.00 depending on the groom's wealth.

I remember the days before my wedding. My future wife, her mother, and her sister were in an expensive jewelry store looking only at the most expensive items. I kept saying that I could not afford such high-priced luxuries which, in my opinion, were not necessary to begin our life together. They ignored every word I said by adding more items to their list. Their arguments over certain items became so fierce that my fiancee's sister, Kobra, grabbed her by the arm, her mother by her black chador, and forced them both out the door. They jumped in a cab, leaving me in the shop with my mouth wide open watching their departure.

I was shocked and embarrassed. I tried to explain to the owner that although I valued my bride more than his whole store, I could not help thinking of the years it would take me to pay the debt for these unnecessary baubles which they desired so much. In the end, I bought her a gold band with diamonds, a gold necklace, a bracelet, and a pair of emerald earrings, all of which equaled a year of my salary.

The groom must also pay for all the expenses of numerous parties and receptions at private clubs chosen by the bride's family. In addition, he has to agree to the amount of *mehriyeh,* a negotiated money for the bride if the marriage were to end in divorce. This has to be settled prior to the wedding, between the groom's family and the parents of the bride. Mehriyeh would be recorded in the marriage certificate to prevent future disputes. It is similar to a prenuptial agreement. The bride's parents may request the payment as part of the wedding formalities regardless of a divorce. Some would invest the money for the bride or use it to avoid its depreciation in future years. In return, the bride's parents would give the newlyweds furniture and bedding. This is called *jahazieh*. It varies from a comforter or a pillow to a car, a house, or furnishing an entire house, depending on the amount of mehriyeh and the wealth of the bride's family.

Unlike American weddings, where all the guests are present to witness the exchange of vows, not every guest in a Persian wedding need be present at the ceremony. Weddings are not held in mosques or religious places but in hotels, clubs, or homes. Therefore, the guests who are not in attendance at the actual wedding, which is held in a separate room or private section with only close friends and relatives present, are in other rooms or outdoors partying, drinking, and celebrating. Liquor, not allowed in Islamic nations, is available from the black market at the right price.

The *mullah*, Moslem clergy, presides over the ceremony by reading from the Koran in Arabic, which most Iranians do not understand. He asks the bride three times if she wants to marry the groom. The bride should not answer "yes" the first time. The groom then presents her with an expensive gift. The bride is asked a second time. According to custom, she still is not supposed to respond. The bridegroom presents her with another gift, more expensive than the first. The question then is asked again. After the third time, if the answer is "yes," the marriage ceremony is completed; if no answer is given, based on the customs, the wedding could be called off.

Because of children playing, running around, screaming, guests talking, telling jokes, drinking, laughing, and generally having a jolly time, the noise or chaos in the background can make it difficult for the anxious bride to hear the Mullah clearly. This causes the bride to become quite nervous. If she cannot hear him, she may miss the last question and the marriage is not official as she did not reply "yes." If she answers too quickly, after the second time, her parents would be upset because she forfeited one of her most expensive presents.

During my wedding, my bride loudly shouted "yes" to the last question to be sure the Mullah heard it, to avoid invalidating the wedding. Her shout scared the daylights out of me. Subsequently, I have seen a few ceremonies at this point become quite hilarious and out of hand.

The newlyweds then return to their respective homes for two weeks. This is called the "Courting Period," which provides the needed time for the bride and the groom to get to know each other better. If either one wishes to change his or her mind, this is the time to back out. The bride and the groom have one last opportunity to decide whether they want to share their lives together. It is not unusual for the bride's family to use this period to assess the dowry given by the groom and to be sure they are satisfied with the total value. There is no need to mention how skillfully everyone must play the game at this critical period.

The families may alter, ignore all or some of these traditions depending on their beliefs, wealth, and education. However, if at all possible, the traditions must be kept.

Receptions are held afterward. Ornately set tables with bouquets of fresh flowers, crystal, and silverware are placed throughout the rooms. Dishes of *Chello kabob*, cooked rice with shish-kabob, fresh fruits, cakes, ice cream, tea, soft drinks and other beverages are served to the guests in enormous quantities. The orchestra plays traditional wedding songs, Persian dancing music, and modern love tunes. Young, beautiful females dance with other ladies while their husbands drink or dance with friends or someone else. At the end of the reception, when the bride and groom are leaving, friends and relatives throw silver coins and rice sugar candies at them. Catching these brings good luck to the unmarried boys and girls in their search for desirable mates.

On my wedding night, Hava's older sister, Kobra, and my sister, Ziba, were appointed by her parents to be the witnesses of the white cloth and proof of her virginity. Family members are appointed to watch over the first few hours of the wedding

72

night. The bridal blood, when the hymen is pierced for the first time, is taken to the parents of the bride on a white cloth. This idea dates back not only to ancient Islamic times, but to Greek mythology as well, as Hymen was the God of marriage.

My wife and I were so exhausted from all the formalities of such a crazy night that we could easily have fallen asleep and not waked up for the next twenty-four hours. But this was out of the question, as we were supposed to do our marital obligation to make her parents happy. We fell on the bed lying on our backs, holding hands trying to regain a little energy to become romantic or at least capable of performing our required duty.

A sudden pounding on the door scared me half to death. It took me a while to pull myself together and make it to the door to find out who needed desperate help from us. There was Kobra, standing with her hands on her hips staring at me, without saying a word. After a minute of silence, she turned to my wife and told her, "Hurry up, get busy there, we don't have all night. Everyone is waiting for me. For Allah's sake get with it, let's go, will you!"

I closed the door, heading to the bathroom to undress. While taking my clothes off, I remembered the sad wedding night of my friend Ata, who was a nice young man but bashful and nervous. His wedding night nearly ruined his marriage because of the stressful situation in which his wedding watchers placed him. It took Ata several nights to be able to consummate his marriage. Every night this agonizing trial would continue, with the watchers knocking on the bedroom door, giving sarcastic advice and heckling the poor guy. It was on the eighth night that the watchers finally were able to go home. But for that entire week, the bride's family only showed impatience, and this made it only more difficult for the poor, young couple.

I was sexually aroused, but wanted to do everything just right. Our wedding night was our first sexual experience together; in fact, it was our first love affair. I wanted it to be

73

perfect for both of us! As we were starting to be loving and romantic, Kobra shouted, "Come on you two, it's time that something happened in there!" I could hear Ziba trying to keep her quiet, giving us the chance to enjoy our time alone. She was telling her, "Sit down; leave them alone; let them enjoy their special time together." Hearing their conversations right behind the door wasn't the best inspiration for romance. With each interruption, we had to start all over again.

Finally, I was ready but Hava became very puzzled, not knowing what was supposed to happen at the moment, which made me even more nervous. Fortunately, with the passion we were feeling for each other, it seemed like all was going well and we were just getting into it when I saw that the stupid white cloth was in the wrong place. With a bit of a struggle I reached for the darn thing, pulled it under her, and we consummated our marriage.

Hava started laughing, crying, then came a little scream for her little performance in that ridiculous circus act. Her sister started making noises by hitting two objects together while screaming and whistling in the middle of the night. Then she wiggled the door knob as though she were coming in. I bounded out of the bed, reached for my robe, and jerked open the door. Kobra looked weird with a big pot and a stick in her hand, continuing her noisemaking act. I gave her the cloth, with a mere whisper of blood on it. It was there, that was all she was waiting for to take to Hava's parents to make them proud. I made a sarcastic remark telling Kobra it wouldn't hurt my feelings if she never came back to my house again.

At the time I was rather disgusted by the preposterous traditional customs. As a more mature man I am sorry for acting irritated because of being young and inexperienced. Through the years I have thought about the old-fashioned cultural tradition, searching for the logic behind it. In all honesty now with an open mind, I respect it and would prefer that young women stay virgins and go through those outdated customs rather than risking having several abortions in their teenage years or suffering from the many incurable sexual diseases of this century. In comparison, it would be much easier to cope with the embarrassment of the noise, white cloth, and banging on the door than having your son or daughter in pain, dying from AIDS because of sexual " freedom."

Although today, love, attraction, and personal choices have important roles in Persian weddings, the wealth of the man still determines which social class the bride would be chosen from. His financial status is an important factor in demanding how educated, young and pretty the bride ought to be. As a matter of fact, in some countries his money could dictate the number of wives he could have A rich, old man can marry any young, beautiful girl he wants or in fact, he can marry more than one wife if he chooses.

Based on Islamic laws, a man can have four permanent, legal wives called *aghdi,* and as many as 76 temporary ones, *sigheh,* at any given time. He may replace one or all of these wives as long as he keeps the limit under the maximum allowed. I often humorously wonder about my wisdom in leaving the old country! Frankly, I believe if a man can survive with one spouse, he should receive a gold medal. Who could possibly handle so many and stay sane or even alive? In preparation for my wedding, a dear friend of mine kept insisting that I should disregard all other qualities in a bride and just look for the most beautiful one. His logic was, all women are alike, why not have a pretty one?

The philosophy and justification behind having more than one wife in Islam, particularly multiple temporary wives, goes back to the Prophet Mohammed, founder of Islam in the sixth century. In short, there are two significant reasons: first, was to encourage men to raise daughters, who were not considered highly prized possessions and often would be buried alive at birth to hide the parents' shame; second, was to provide financial support for unmarried women, particularly single mothers without income. This privilege satisfied male chauvinism and gave them a feeling of superiority. In a way, temporary wives play the role of legal girlfriends and give some women a way to sell or barter their bodies for food and shelter. Their children however, were not entitled to the father's estate if he didn't give specific directions for them in his will. Each permanent wife and daughter, according to Islamic law, received one share of the estate while sons were entitled to two.

I cannot remember any clear rule on the amount of money, love, time, and attention a husband was to devote to his temporary wives. However, Islamic doctrine dictated specific rules for taking more than one permanent wife. The standards are so strict that in fact they make it nearly impossible to have more than one wife. Moslem men often interpreted this religious doctrine to fit their own personal needs. Thus, through the years, they have skillfully modified the true requirements to continue having multiple spouses. The original law states: "The only way a man can acquire more than one wife is, if he can be equal to each wife in every aspect of his life." Such equality means emotionally, morally, financially, and the amount of time devoted to each one. A true interpretation means: no multiple wives, because it is almost impossible for humans to love and treat four people equally at the same time.

Men in a clever way have been able to modify this law and consider the equality only in terms of financial matters. A rich man who could purchase each wife an equally priced home, identical Mercedes, drivers, maids, and other necessities had no problem having his multiple wives. He would spend one week a month with each wife and consider it fair and equitable for having four wives. Emotionally, he tries to be equally nice to each one in order to receive the best treatment in bed, plus good manners and kindness brought the husband the most delicious food in each house and more! One would assume that those who naturally have a terrible personality would act nasty to all, to be emotionally fair to each one.

On the other end of the scale, a poor man living in a single room would divide his room into four equal sections and call it fair to justify his four wives, the way Prophet Mohammed asked him to do. Ironically, to prove equality in every way, he may send his wives to work in the fields to bring four paychecks home. His job would be supervising the wives by sitting on his "tush" all day in a tea house, smoking his pipe, and playing backgammon with the other men.

I would like to share an interesting article on "Cultures Clash in Nebraska" from the Rocky Mountain News, December 2, 1996. My intention is not to defend the people involved or blame the American legal system. It is merely to make a point that culture is a concrete foundation of human life which creates bases for behavior. In a new life and new country, it becomes a major source of confusion as one attempts to adjust.

"The proud father of six was beaming on Nov. 9 when more than 100 fellow Iraqi refugees crowded into his house and the house next door for the wedding of his two eldest daughters. The male guests gathered in one house, the females in the other. A Muslim cleric from Ohio was flown in. For the Iraqis, it was the social event of the year. For the police, it was a crime. The authorities say the father forced his 13 and 14-year-old daughters into marrying two countrymen more than twice their age. The men took their brides to their homes and consummated the marriages. When the older girl ran away with a boyfriend a few days later, the father and the girl's husband went to the police and said they wanted her back. Instead in a conflict between old-country culture and American justice, the girls were taken into protective custody, and the father and the men he considered his sons-in-law were arrested."

The father was charged with two counts of child abuse and faced up to one year in the Lancaster County Jail. His wife was charged with contributing to the delinquency of minors. The grooms have been charged with rape. Each faces up to 50 years in prison.

77

What we have here is an example of a cultural gulf. The grooms could not understand why they were arrested. They didn't think that they had done anything wrong as there was no intent to break the law. The father contends that his daughters willingly married the men and that his family had only been following their ancient traditions of arranged marriages in their new homeland, a place where they thought people were free to practice their religion without fear of the police or prosecutors. The father was only doing what he thought was in the best interests of his daughters. He was devastated!

At the heart of this case is the clash of the culture of newcomers with American mores and laws. It is a conflict shrouded in issues of multiculturalism and ignorance of the ways of a strange new world.

Taking care of their children, helping them to secure a promising future by selecting the best possible partners for their sons or daughters are at the very heart of Islamic society.

Another interesting cultural point about the Middle East is whether or not people are telling you what they *really* think. At times, I have felt that people from this region have a theatrical attitude toward life, as if they are on stage, always acting. It's a stratagem for protecting private thoughts and feelings and has come to be a permanent institution, with a name of its own. In Farsi, it is known as *ketman,* which in a way means cover-up. It has become almost a game, and one never knows if the truth is being told or not. Another way of understanding the meaning is, as we say in America, "don't hang out your dirty laundry in public." It is amazing how consistently almost everyone in the Middle East follows the custom.

My siblings were upset with me for describing in this book memories I had of our abusive father. In my defense I asked them: "Did I lie about him or were my words actual facts?" Their reply was: "He is our father; you should never write anything like this to complete strangers!" I also have not been very popular with some of my fellow countrymen for writing some facts about life in Iran, as many believed my words, which were based on true reflections, were demeaning to the country.

I would like to conclude this chapter by writing about three personal experiences and unforgettable stories demonstrating the importance of understanding the differences between the cultures of the East and the West.

It begins with my meeting an interesting, inquisitive, fun-loving American basketball coach, Don McCanniki, while working at Ahwaz Gondi-shappor University. Sadly, I cannot remember the correct spelling of his last name. At the time we met, I was the athletic director at the University and one of few who spoke English. Don insisted that he wanted me to be his translator and before I knew it, I was appointed to this position. I liked him immediately as he was a wonderful American, full of humanity, kindness, compassion, and endowed with a great sense of humor. The Iranian girls liked him even more, because he was a tall, good-looking, blond bachelor with impeccable manners.

Don and I took several trips together to various parts of the country with our athletic teams. I had a wonderful opportunity to practice my English and he was curious and intrigued with the Iranian culture and customs. He had learned that I was honest and straight forward in my answers to his questions, and that *ketman* was not part of my character or who I was.

With his sense of risk-taking and adventure, he unknowingly at times placed me in several awkward, or better said, scary situations. Because we had become close friends, we often liked to joke with one another, and I still have many fond memories of the times we spent in each other's company. These memories bring a smile to my face.

Once, for the National Collegiate Championship Games, we went to Mashhad, capital of Iran's northeast border province of Khorassan. For Shia Moslems, when one talks about Mashhad one talks not so much about a place as of a spiritual experience. Mashhad is the rainbow's end, the fulfillment of dreams. It is a place of miracles where the impossible can be possible.

The reason for Mashhad's magnetism as a holy place and a very important religious site is because it is here that the tomb of Imam Reza is located. Imam Reza died in the ninth century and he was the eighth and last Shia Imam. Of all the Shia Imams, or saints after Ali, the Prophet Mohammand's son-in-law, Imam Reza is the most loved and revered.

Of course, Don wanted to see the inside of the shrine. Now, if he had been in America, this would not have been a problem. But we were not. There are many sacred places in Iran that non-Moslems, or infidels, are not allowed to visit and this shrine is definitely one of those places. I refused to take him, knowing how serious the consequences could be. His presence would be considered disrespectful and "unclean."

But no matter how many times I warned Don and advised him that this was not a good idea, I could not convince him. He had read in an Iranian travel magazine an advertisement about Mashhad, an ad that was quite misleading:

"Whoever goes to Mashhad on pilgrimage, God will surely destine to Paradise, and his body will be forbidden to the flames of Hell; and whoever goes there with sorrow, God will take his sorrow away."

With his American way of thinking, he could not understand why I was so adamant about his not going and probably thought that I was joking with him. But, believe me, I was seriously concerned about his safety. I knew the culture and I knew the people! Religious tombs are very sacred places where typically thousands of people are visiting and praying. All they would need to do is see an infidel American and they would begin to spit on him in disgust. Soon he would be drowning in spit!

Don did not accept my words of caution and sought out our host from Mashhad. The host, being a true Iranian, never

80

wanting to hurt anyone's feelings and always trying to be accommodating (and, of course, let us not forget *ketman*) said that he would take Don through the back doors into the tomb. There would not be a problem! This was all Don wanted to hear, and I could not change his mind. Therefore, against my better judgment, I ended up going with him because I knew someone had to safeguard him.

We silently entered through the first two archways with no problem. But soon I noticed that the Moslem worshippers were staring at this 6 foot 4 inch white male humming under his breath "do, do, do...," while gawking at everything with eyes wide open. It terrified me, not knowing what was going to happen next.

For as long as I can remember, I have been very fortunate in that God has given me the gift of being quick to respond to awkward or difficult situations. This blessed sixth sense has come in handy and has enabled me to pull myself out of some uncomfortable circumstances. So, without a second thought, I elbowed Don and told him to imitate me and do exactly what I did. The looks on the worshipper's faces must have scared him, because he did not hesitate or ask any questions.

Whenever I kneeled and kissed the ground, he did the same and when I prayed out loud reciting "La Elaha El lalah," he mimicked me and said "La. la lah," not knowing what in the world it meant or what he was doing. Suddenly, I noticed the crowd had changed. The disgusted looks turned to admiration. Some started asking me what was going on with this stranger? I replied that he wanted to marry my sister, and the only way we would accept him as an in-law was if he became a Moslem. After that, we were given royal treatment and warmly welcomed in town, even receiving free lunches in several restaurants.

I truly have no idea what might have happened to us, or more specifically to Don, if I had not been able to think so quickly on my feet.

My final trip with Don was a year later to the modern city

of Shiraz, near what was the capital of the ancient Persian Empire, Persepolis. It is known as the city of wine, roses, and nightingales, and Shiraz spreads out like an immense garden on a green plain. It's rich in historic monuments with an agreeable climate, and in the spring the city comes alive with the smell of orange-blossoms. The people are known for their charm and hospitality.

We were in Shiraz for a week for the National Collegiate Championship Games. Don was more than excited and happy, because he was hoping to continue in a more serious way his friendship with the beautiful Zohreh, to whom he had been introduced a year ago in Mashhad. Don was impressed with this lovely city, its magnificent gardens, and friendly residents, but he was more interested in the gorgeous Persian girl with deep, brown eyes framed with long dark eyelashes. She was the captain of the girls volleyball team at Pahlavi University in Shiraz, and she had a strong, supple, athletic body.

Don and Zohreh had been secretly communicating throughout the year and you know "who" had to translate the letters. All I can say is that my friend was head over heels in love and infatuated with Zohreh. He was 28 and she was 20. I tried to caution him and slow him down, knowing that although Iran was considered Western (in the 1960's), and girls wore short skirts and make-up, the social mores and customs were still of the old ways.

But, I too was a romantic and I only hoped for the best. Sadly, for my dear friend Don, he couldn't spend any time alone with Zohreh because young girls are not permitted to be alone in public with a male companion or have any physical contact. Even holding hands was frowned upon. Of course, under the present Islamic government, any contact is forbidden. Young people must always be under supervision or have a private place to meet in secret. Therefore, whenever Don and Zohreh met, they had to be accompanied by her older sister as Zohreh could not leave the house on her own.

Their second problem was language. Don knew very little

Farsi, and Zohreh's English was just as limited. So, they not only had her older sister tagging along, but they also needed me to translate.

The third problem had nothing to do with Don or Zohreh, but with her sister, who had taken a liking to me. Shohreh was even more striking than her younger sister; however, I was married and had no interest in an affair.

Now, if you will permit me to digress, I must explain that Middle Eastern women are very strong willed with a mind of their own. Contrary to Western thought and their secondary role in society, they still somehow manage to get almost everything that they want. For instance, in Afghanistan under the cruel Taliban regime, women were forced to wear burkas under which they cunningly hid books and cameras, the former to continue their education in secret, the latter to document for the future the atrocities committed. These women are very clever, and although considered second-class, are extremely smart in knowing how to outwit the system and the men. As strange as it may seem to a Westerner, many of them would rather wear the burka than not, because they become invisible, and others cannot recognize who is coming out of whose house!

But no matter how many times I said, "no" to Shohreh, she persisted. She would not mind being my second wife or my mistress! She was upset with me for not being much of a man and meeting her expectations. Unfortunately, her bitterness turned to spitefulness, and often Zohreh could not meet Don because her sister would not accompany her.

These frustrations aside, the highlight of our visit to Shiraz was an invitation to an authentic Middle Eastern lunch at a traditional Persian family's home. The two sisters were thrilled that Don wanted to experience this memorable occasion, and they insisted that their home would be the best place.

I just about had a heart attack knowing the grave consequences if Don innocently did something to offend the family. Truly, I did not know how they would be able to convince their parents to invite us to their house without a problem.

Don could not stop jumping up and down with joy. His efforts to have a relationship with Zohreh was terrifying enough for me, but going to her home and meeting the family, scared me beyond words. The sisters and Don were delighted and simply ignored my feelings of fear and nervousness. I could not change Don's mind, and I consequently spent the next two sleepless nights worrying about everything.

We dressed in our best clothes, as a common sign of respect to the host, and drove to one of the most prestigious residential areas of Shiraz. Two maids, one younger, the other an old, homely looking hag with a patch over one eye, brought us slippers, as it is customary to take off one's shoes upon entering a home as well as all religious places.

We were introduced to a gracious hostess, their mother, a well dressed and dignified grandmother, and to their stately, educated, handsome father.

Their home was absolutely beautiful with many colorful, antique Persian rugs. It was obvious that they were a wealthy family, and the father's important governmental position complemented their fortune. There were many gold, silver, and bronze antique statues and vases, and the furniture was all hand carved and exquisite. A gold sword embedded with large diamonds and rubies on the handle caught Don's eye, and he wanted to know more about it. I quietly assured him that when the time was right, I would ask her father and he would tell us the story behind it.

Don was impressed with the house and the family. The aroma from the kitchen made his mouth water. Yet, his main focus was on Zohreh. He was mesmerized by her beauty. Under my breath, I whispered to him not to be a rubberneck in following her every move but to keep his head down in respect to the father.

After the formalities of the introductions and some polite, small talk, Don looked around and asked me with a puzzled look on his face, " Where are we going to eat this wonderful

Persian meal?" I answered," On the floor." Thinking that I was kidding him, he gave me a funny look. Then he saw the maids spread a large white linen tablecloth over the Persian rug. He shook his head and raised his eyebrows in surprise. Immediately, the females of the house set the dishes, the silverware, goblets, and candlesticks on the tablecloth. It was a nicer setting than any dining table Don had ever seen.

The younger maid held an antique, oblong-shaped basin in front of Don and stood next to him with a decorated brass water pitcher (*Aftabeh lagan*). Don looked at me quizzically and asked "What is this for?" I quickly replied, "To wash your hands." Surprisingly, he said, "Do they think that I am so dirty that I have to wash my hands?" I answered "No, just do it, please." Then he continued, "Do they think I'm lazy and cannot walk to the washroom?" My answer was: "It is the custom and the traditional way, and that is what you wanted to experience. Please, don't embarrass me by asking too many questions; just do as I say." The maid then proceeded with the basin to the next in honor, me, and then to the head of the household and the rest of the family according to their rank of importance.

The Persian feast consisted of *fesanjon*, a sort of stew made of chicken breast, walnuts, onion, and pomegranate sauce served over Basamati rice with saffron, *tahdig,* the buttery brown potatoes at the bottom of the pot of rice, *kabob*, broiled meats, *gormeh sabzi,* another kind of stew with meat, potatoes, kidney beans and green vegetables, *garni yarikh,* stuffed eggplant, cucumber and garlic yogurt salad, fresh bread, and *torhsi*, pickled vegetables.

In Iran just about every vegetable and half the fruits are made into pickles. This delicacy is to Iranians what wine is to the Frenchman. No good meal is complete without them and, when a prominent guest is being entertained, the host breaks out a specially precious bottle of good vintage pickles which have been lovingly stored in the cellar for years. That night we were served three torshis!

Don was overwhelmed and intrigued by it all and asked the father a million questions. All I wanted to do was partake of this delicious food, but I had to translate first from English to Farsi and then from Farsi to English. Don was giving me indigestion!

He kept rolling his eyes toward the jeweled, gold sword hanging on the wall behind the father, giving me a hint that he wanted to know the history of it. Originally belonging to his great grandfather, a famous warlord, the sword, the prize possession of the family, had been passed down from generation to generation. With great pride, the father stood up, took the sword off the wall, and began to expound on every detail about this special sword; meanwhile, his and my lunch were getting cold. Then he ever so gently put it on the carpet next to the tablecloth.

I was exhausted having to translate every single word of the conversation, so I decided to ignore Don's never ending questions and enjoy my delicious lunch. To be polite to both parents, I continued to answer or translate, but in the briefest way possible. A simple "yes " or "no." Mr. Amiri asked Don if he liked the Iranian meal? Don, who had learned some Farsi, understood the question himself and replied *baleh*, meaning yes. Then he asked me to please tell them that "this was the best meal he ever tasted."

Then, being the practical joker that I am, I decided to play a game with him as he often did with me. I began with asking Don, "Did you hear me saying no, a few times?" He answered, "Yes, I did." Then with a serious face, I said to him, " Did I hear you correctly that you replied 'yes' to their father when he asked you if you enjoyed the Persian dishes. He responded, "Of course I did!"

I told him, this was what I was afraid of and I apologized for forgetting to tell him about one important custom in my country. If a man liked the meal, he must make love to the cook to express his appreciation. Finally, Don stopped talking for a few minutes and I was able to finish my lunch in peace. After his shock, with hope in his heart, he said: "Zohreh, must have been the cook." I laughed and replied "You wish!"

Just then, the ugly, old maid with the one good eye walked in to pick up the leftovers and tablecloth. I rolled my eyes toward her with a grin on my face. He just about lost his breath for a minute, then said, "No, you must be kidding me!" Knowing that I had him in the palm of my hand, I gently replied, "I wish I was." He did not say another word.

Nervously, he said, "I don't mind the mother; I can handle even the grandmother, but not that scary lady." Frightened, he asked, "Why didn't Mr. Amiri put his sword back on the wall?" I told him, "This is a very important custom and he wants to make sure that the job is done right; otherwise, he will use it to cut off your manhood!"

Meanwhile, as soon as the tablecloth, plates, food, and silverware were picked up, the women brought pillows, sheets and blankets for us. Frozen in place, he looked at me with huge green eyes. I thought that I had teased him enough and said, "I was kidding, they just want us to take a nap." He was puzzled again and asked, "Don't these people have any work to do that they eat and sleep right afterward?" I laughed and told him, "You were the one who asked for an authentic traditional way, not me. And this is it!"

After the nap, they served us tea in the most delicate, small crystal glasses and pastry on Limoge plates. We both thanked them from the bottom of our hearts for being so gracious and going through all this trouble. Mr. and Mrs. Amiri both at the same time replied, "Oh, this was nothing compared to the job you have offered our daughter." Hearing that shocked me, thinking, what job offer? Before I could say anything, Zohreh, standing behind them, made a face that signaled me to not say a word. So, I politely shook hands with her parents and said, "She deserves it." Then we departed without any further words or my translating to Don what had just transpired. He would never understand it, and I didn't want to hurt his feelings. The real reason for inviting us to their home and lavishing us with such a fine meal was a *ketman*. It would have crushed him to have known that their hospitality was staged.

Don was one of the most influential people in encouraging me to come to America. I missed him a great deal after he left Iran. We lost contact with each other, but in my heart I always hope that we will meet once again. Regardless of how many times I have told this story, writing about it still makes me laugh. It's as if it only happened yesterday.

President Clinton's scandal with women reminded me of another valuable piece of advice my grandmother gave us. In Moslem countries, the penalties for messing around with someone's wife or daughter are quite severe. They consider it destroying their family honor, with only death or castration being the way of protecting that honor. Her advice was quite proper in saying, "A smart man would never allow his penis to chop his head."

Thinking about her wisdom and watching the news each day made me wonder if that little amount of fooling around was worth a possible loss of the Presidency of the United States for President Clinton.

I remember once, watching TV during the Camp David talks when the media were questioning Mr. Clinton and Yassir Arafat. I detected a look of fear on Arafat's face and his eyes seemed to be dilated eyes. My observation was that he definitely was thinking about the sex scandal, and wondering if President Clinton would be around long enough to sign the peace agreement. Surely in his Middle Eastern mind he was not certain whether Monica's father would kill the President to defend his daughter's honor!

I have one final humorous story to share. Bob Mathias, former American athlete who won the 1956 decathlon Olympic Gold medal, was hired as a track coach by the Iranian Olympic Committee.

One day, looking like a chicken with its head cut off, Bob was racing back and forth across the field, training many athletes on the track team in their variety of events (runners, jumpers, throwers, hurdlers, pole vaulters, etc.) General Pooyan, chief of the Shah's police, who was at the field every day making a nuisance of himself, told Bob in Farsi, "I want you to make my son the best runner on the Iranian Olympic team," a theme he repeated every day. In fact, Bob was hoping to throw his son Ali off the team for not having the same athletic ability as the other members. He had no idea that Ali was placed there, not because of his own ability, but because of his father's position. Thus, Bob would not be permitted to do so.

Bob's personal translator was busy, so he turned to me and asked me to help out. I gladly agreed, until I heard what he wanted me to say.

He said to me, "Would you please tell this moron that a horse is a horse and a mule is a mule; no matter how hard I train his son, I cannot make a horse out of a mule!"

I paused for a moment, thinking that this would create a major problem. First, I did not want to spend the rest of my young life in prison for the crime of translating Bob's words. Second, I was concerned for what would happen to Bob. I expeditiously responded to the General, "Mr. Mathias believes that your son has great potential. He could easily be a medal winner in the international games, but we must leave him alone to mature gradually. If you push him harder than necessary, it might be detrimental to his future, and possibly not winning a future, international Gold Medal!"

The General was thrilled to hear this. He shook Bob's hand and said, "Thank you, thank you!" Bob gave me a questioning look and asked, "Why is he thanking me? I just told him off." I answered, "He is thanking the wrong man. He should have been thanking me for saving your ass from going to jail. I beg of you, please show only the utmost respect to those of authority in this country, because you never know what they will do to you. This is not America. The rules of justice, law, and order are exclusively in the hands of the officials who run the country.

The author receiving a gift from the late Shah in
recognition for winning the National Championship
title in track and field and soccer

90

CHOOSING AMERICA

"Why did you come to America?" I have been asked this question so many times that it makes this chapter easy to write. My reasons were much more involved than one simple answer. Often I changed the subject or gave a quick reply, such as, my graduate education. After three and a half decades, I now have time to respond in depth. My answer is twofold, but posed in the form of two questions. First, why did I want to escape from Iran, and second, why did I choose the United States?

Ever since I can remember, I had wanted to run away from home. However, I knew it was not a good idea, as I had no place to run to. By the tenth grade I came up with this crazy idea of not only running away from home but escaping the whole darn country. I thought I could erase my past and start a new life. I explored every possible way, including working for a cruise line or on a cargo ship. However, none of my wishful ideas came to fruition. Later on, I thought my athletic career would be a good way out if I could defect while our team was competing in a foreign country. The problem was that the police state in Iran did not allow such an opportunity as the coaches always had our passports in their possession.

Under the Shah's dictatorship, obtaining a passport to get out of Iran required so much bribe money that I could never afford it. Furthermore, even if I could get a passport, the chance of my getting a visa to any country was next to impossible. The other major hurdle was finding a country which would grant me permanent residency.

During my early twenties there never was a day of my life that I did not plan my final exit. No matter where I was or what I was doing, I dreamt of a future new country. Soccer, being popular in Europe, made Italy, Germany, Holland, and Austria my top choices. It gave me hope of earning a lucrative income if I trained hard and was good enough to play in their professional circle. However, not knowing Italian, German, or Dutch was a major problem. In addition, I was told that people native to those countries were not receptive to foreigners living there. My next preference was Greece, as it had always been one of my favorite countries. The culture, people, food, and music are similar to those of my homeland, and it's a democratic nation, but the chances of making a living in Greece didn't look promising either. I did not know Greek and could not picture myself as a fisherman or sheep herder. Besides Farsi, Turkish, and Armenian, one of the languages I thought I knew was English. So, in 1960 I started thinking of America as my dreamland for a new home. It became a more definite plan after my college graduation in 1961.

I knew my immigration process to the United States was going to take time, but I never imagined it would take seven years! As a young, skillful player who had high hopes of playing professional soccer, I knew by the time I would be admitted into the U.S.A. my playing years would be over. Wisely, I began thinking of coaching as a career.

In addition to my unhappy childhood, there were five other reasons which propelled me to want to escape Iran. These gave me the determination that I needed.

One: Being a man with some vision for the future, I foresaw the hopeless years ahead for Iranians. I read the signs on the wall before many people noticed them and knew that a democratic government would not be in the forecast for a predictable future. Many of my friends were too involved in making money to notice where the country was heading. I took the risk of taking my family away from a society that had no values for human rights and I was ready and willing to accept the possible consequences. Americans, along with other citizens of free nations, cannot begin to understand how horrible it is to live with prohibitive restrictions and no freedom. Whether living under the Shah's police state, under strict Islamic rules, or under any other dictatorship, if one is not able to read a desired book, watch a T.V. program, listen to music, or speak freely and write without censorship, it isn't a life worth living!

I was lucky to get away at the time I did as it is practically impossible to obtain a passport to exit Iran now. I declined a dream job offer in 1974, a job which most Iranians would have given an arm or a leg for. I wanted no part in that government. Many thought I had lost my mind and some honestly cried for me. That was the first time my wife, Hava, insisted I seek professional help. Everyone told me how stupid I was, leaving when my future seemed so good. A few friends came up with various creative approaches to convince me to stay. I heard these routine, common statements over and over. "We are not telling you not to go, we are just asking you to stay a while longer, two or three years to make your millions, then go where you wish." Counting on collecting sizable amounts of bribe money from my anticipated important future positions was what they were talking about.

I had absolutely no interest in further conversations of that kind. Regardless of where we went or who we visited, there were numerous hours of long, heated discussions. Most were initiated by Hava in her continuous attempt to change my mind. The advice from all was clear: Don't bad mouth the system; go along with them; collect what belongs to you, meaning take a government job and accept as much bribe money as you can, then take off. No need to leave permanently, to lose your job. Make your millions quickly; buy vacation homes around the world, and enjoy your time away from Iran. But be sure to leave the door open to return and make more money.

My repeated reply was the same: "You be the millionaires cheating and stealing from your countrymen; I am going to find a life with freedom and happiness." I went on, insulting them at times by saying, "How can you call *roshveh,* bribes, your own personal assets with the right to collect?"

Two: I never felt as if I fit in with the others. Although I have the greatest respect and admiration for the Persian culture, heritage, and people, I somehow felt different. As strange as it may sound, I always felt out of place in Iran. I praise the strong character of Persians for surviving throughout history, suffering defeats and destruction at the hands of Arabs, Alexander the Great, and the Mongolians. Because of their strong character, I hope Iranians will be able to build a new democratic country, regardless of how hard it may be, in order to enjoy a free life. Looking back, I feel especially indebted to my loyal fans who supported me during the most memorable events of my sports career, and afterwards, as athletics was my only salvation during those years. I love my family and friends dearly. I miss my teammates with whom I grew up, traveled, and shared many exciting, happy, and sad moments. But all in all, I never quite felt comfortable or truly part of that restrictive society.

Perhaps my family background played a big role in my feeling alien to my birth place, or perhaps it was because my parents and siblings were not devoted Moslems, attending the mosque regularly or praying like the rest of the citizens. Also, possibly being too honest to adapt to the corrupt ways of accepting bribes put me in an awkward position. Whatever the reasons, I always felt a stranger in my own country. I cared too much for the ordinary citizens to the point that their pain, torture, hunger, and sadness made me suffer with them. I couldn't take a bribe from anyone, believing it was stealing from the disadvantaged. And finally, I couldn't agree with their belief, "If you don't want to be sorry, you must adapt to the color of the crowd." In Farsi, the saying is: *"Khahi na-shavi rosva, ham- rangeh jama-at sho."*

Three: Seeking freedom became a lifelong goal for me. Democracy doesn't have as much value for some people as it has for me. I have met Americans who do not appreciate this great gift given to them at birth. They have no idea what a wonderful life they are blessed with, simply by living in a democratic country. For me, it was a constant struggle to obtain such a life. Unless one has been in a similar situation, it is difficult to understand my emotions. Life under a true dictatorship can provide a completely different meaning and context for the word "freedom." I was so determined to have my freedom that I was willing to go to any extent.

Four: My athletic trips to Europe allowed me to witness a new way of life and freedom, which added yet another reason for my decision. The trips opened my eyes, by making me realize that my dreams of living in a free country were not just figments of my imagination but were real. Once in Paris, while visiting the Eiffel Tower, I lost several hours of consciousness. Strangely enough, I did not pass out or become sick; I just lost my connection with the world around me, not knowing where I was, what I was doing, or who I was. It was the most exciting and satisfying feeling I have ever had. Thinking about my past, how I had survived, how I was in France, and where I would be in the future made me lose my sense of awareness. I believe my numbness also came from not knowing how I was going to escape Iran or where I could go to be protected from the SAVAK. Not having the answers, plus the excitement of being in a free country, caused an unusual feeling of blankness. I never could figure out why it happened nor exactly how long my memory lapse lasted.

Five: Working with Americans in Iran helped me make the final decision. This was probably the most influential factor in coming to America. I was the athletic director for the University of Gondishapoor in Ahwaz, the second largest university in Iran. My other duties included Dean of Students at the Ahwaz Agriculture College. The college was administered by a joint venture, Iran's Ministry of Higher Education and the Near East Foundation, an American company based in New York. The academic dean, along with 30 percent of our staff, were from the U.S. Some of the Americans were the best ambassadors of their country, gaining the highest respect from all Iranians they dealt with. A few, unfortunately, were rather embarrassing representatives of America.

I met several American friends at Ahwaz Agriculture College and those who recognized my potential kept encouraging me to come to America. They insisted that I get my doctorate in order to obtain better positions in Iran as doctoral titles were the best tools for advancement. My American friends knew nothing about my plans for making America my new home.

Admission to the U.S. took seven years of paperwork, testing, preparation, and documents fulfilling formalities. Because of the enormous hardship the Iranian government placed on me by not issuing a passport, plus the U.S. requirements for admittance, I thought by the time I made it to my new country I would be eligible for admission to a nursing home. However, I was so determined that it didn't matter how long it might take, even if my arrival coincided with my funeral. I knew, if I made it out of Iran, I would find a way to stay in America.

Even though I received acceptances from other American universities, I chose the University of Wyoming since they offered me a financial scholarship first. It is important at this juncture to express how grateful I am to the late Dr. Burns and his wonderful wife, Agnes, from Laramie, Wyoming. Through their diligent efforts I received my acceptance at the University of Wyoming and it is they who were instrumental in securing a graduate teaching and coaching assistantship for me. Without financial assistance, it would not have been possible to pursue my education and support a family in America. I didn't have sufficient knowledge about America to know the specific differences between each state or geographical region. I envisioned the United States as being all the same, a great place to live free, land of unlimited opportunities with little climatic differences.

Wyoming proved to be an interesting choice as I did not have a clue as to what to expect or the differences between Laramie, Los Angeles, or Las Vegas. I was too excited to worry about the minor details in distinguishing between Wyoming, California, or Nevada. I was just thrilled to come to America!

My problems in making such a major move included an additional twist, making our exit from Iran even more complicated. Hava was steadfastly against it. She persistently caused enormous heartaches, creating an unbearable life at home. Regardless of what kind of obstacles or their number, I took my time and kept leaping over them one at a time in order to reach the finish line. In hopes of a better life, I succeeded in getting my wife and daughter out. To leave Iran today is an even greater monumental task. Those who did not notice what lay ahead had their tails caught in the lucrative system and suddenly it became too late. Some of my friends, who saved millions but were trapped, have precious little to spend their wealth on now.

Thinking about the friends and relatives who tried to prevent me from leaving leaves me with mixed feelings, a sense of accomplishment tempered with sadness. Tragically, after the Revolution, some of the same friends and relatives were executed. The ones who were not had only two choices: leave their home, money, belongings, and flee for their lives; or stay and suffer the consequences. Those choosing the latter, with their millionaire status, have no life. The so-called "millionaires" must stand in line for rations like everyone else. Their other choice is to purchase the items in the black market at astronomical prices.

Imagine a pound of meat as expensive as $150 and a carton of milk or eggs for $30! Truly, having millions under these conditions would not appeal to me. I would much prefer to be poor but happy and free.

The ones who fled in a hurry left without their fortunes accumulated over so many years. Many have unhappy lives in their new country because of not being able to adapt on low incomes. Others, who were more fortunate in somehow taking their money out, were forced to leave their material possessions behind in the rush for freedom. It is ironic to think how some of them had given me advice to be smart and stay in Iran with the prospects of becoming a multimillionaire.

My friend's advice about collecting money reminded me of my first experience with a bribe, an experience which I never could get out of my mind. It happened five years before I came to America in 1962 in Khorramshahr, which is one of the major cities in the province of Khoosistan. It is an important, busy seaport on the Persian Gulf located on the north of Shatt al Arab River west of the city of Abadan, Iran and Basra, Iraq.

I had been given the position of superintendent of physical education, recreation, and athletics. Because of the tariffs collected on imports and exports, Khorramshahr, after Tehran, had the largest financial budget in the country.

Most government employees had to pay an inordinate amount of bribes, *roshveh,* to the important officials in Tehran to get a job in Khorramshahr. Fortunately, I did not have to pay anything, as I was given the position because no one else was qualified to do my work.

The climate of the entire province is semiarid and it is hot and humid, very much like parts of Iraq. At the time, all sport activities were performed outdoors in the oppressive heat and humidity, often combined with rain, sand, and mosquitos.

It was my brainstorm to build a gymnasium with air conditioning, proper lighting, and seating for 4,000 people to promote as many athletic events in the city as possible. After soccer, the most popular sports in Iran were volleyball, wrestling, basketball, and weight lifting. My dream was to build an indoor sports arena for the athletes so that they could excel in these sports the best possible way.

It took me two years to complete the formalities for the building, including the approval of the budget and obtaining permission from numerous government, state, and city officials, in regard to specs, use and conditions. I had to jump through so many hoops, that at times, I wondered if it was even worth all the time and effort, but I was determined and I did it.

One day, early in the construction phase, the owner of the company who had won the bid, said to me that he had some urgent business to take care of with me. Breathing down my neck, he said that he needed to come to my house and discuss some issues. My office was available as a meeting place, but he insisted that he wanted to talk to me in a more private place. I brushed him off, as I found him weird and offensive. I had no interest in inviting him to my home and had no idea what business he would have with me. Therefore, I kept putting him off. I ignored him as much as possible. Full of enthusiasm, the construction of our gymnasium began and everything continued on schedule.

I hired two "watchers" for roughly one U.S. dollar a day, higher than the going rate at the time in Iran to be my informers and oversee the project close up. It was their job to report to me if they noticed anything unusual and out of the ordinary.

One afternoon the watchers came running to my office to tell me that the contractors were pouring dirt into the foundation instead of cement and mixing it with the concrete. I was so upset that I rushed to the site and kicked them out. I could not believe that anyone with a conscious could possibly do something like this, as earthquakes are quite common in Iran.

That night, Mr. Khalili, the owner of the construction company came to my house apologizing, not for his company's cheating, but rather for his being unable to meet with me sooner. He handed me a briefcase full of cash as "hush money" with a promise that more would be coming to me at the end, if only I turned a blind eye to what would be happening with the construction! Sickened by his proposal, I threw him and his briefcase out of my house. I can only guess how much money he was offering to me when he opened the briefcase. I could not think how much he was planning on siphoning from the building of that gymnasium contract. I was unaware of how their system works at the time, but I soon learned that this was a common practice in Iran for all government contracts. Every highway and many government projects were built with substandard materials depending on the amount of kickbacks the officials could skim off the top.

Early the next morning, I was summoned to the governor's office. Mr. Aziz was a distinguished-looking gentleman with graying hair and mustache. He ordered everyone out of his office and sent for tea. He offered me a chair next to his desk, and he began to lavish praise on me and my accomplishments. He told me that he thought of me as a son. Then, he added, "I know how young and inexperienced you are. I would like to give you some fatherly advice, and I will only do this once. Do you understand me, my son? If you are smart, you will accept your share of the "profit," and say nothing. This way, we all can go on with our lives, and you will not interfere with us and the system. If you do otherwise, I promise you that you will be sorry. Have I made myself clear to you?"

I could not believe my ears. To make sure that I had not misunderstood this powerful governor I asked, "Sir, are you suggesting that I take the contractor's money, and let him pour dirt into the foundation instead of cement?" He nodded his head in agreement and responded, "You are an intelligent boy, you figure it out." I answered him, " I am sorry, but I cannot do that." He replied, "I told you that I am only going to tell you this once! You are excused to leave. This meeting is over."

The following morning, I received a telegraph from His Majesty in Tehran, referring to me as Parviz the "Problem Solver," and stating that I was needed in the capital city immediately for an important assignment. His Majesty requesting my immediate presence in Tehran made my mind race, thinking about the possible positions the Shah was going to offer me.

I was put on a plane that evening heading for Tehran to meet with His Majesty ASAP. I never was given an audience with His Majesty, but instead I was taken to the city of Rasht, north of Tehran to mediate a conflict between the teachers and the administration in that city. After that I was flown from one city to another for the next three or four months without really knowing what my purpose was. Afterward they sent me back to Khorramshar, and the gymnasium was completed! I guess the title bestowed on me the "Problem Solver" was the correct one, as I solved all their problems by being out of their way!

Escaping my country, in which freedom had no meaning, was what I did. Luckily I left in 1967, having prepared myself for a timely exit. Finding a new life and freedom in America was what I had dreamed of and envisioned all my young life. Visiting the Statue of Liberty, which I have done many times, has made me simultaneously the saddest and the happiest of persons. I feel sad for all the people living under repression. My happiness comes from having been determined in my convictions and for having followed them through. It certainly paid off to be persistent, not letting others or seemingly insurmountable obstacles change my mind. I am full of joy tasting the fruit of my dreams. Knowing that my children will never have to live under the dictatorship and the corruption which I endured is truly a priceless possession.

Many months prior to our departure were spent listening to people who meant well, giving me their "knowledgeable" advice about Americans. All were enthusiastic, giving seriously considered opinions. As a polite Persian I had to listen, pretending to give them my full attention; otherwise, I would have offended them. They wanted to be certain I knew what life in America, particularly Wyoming, would be like. Cowboys lived there, they said, as they had seen many a John Wayne movie. If they did not like the way you talked or dressed, they could shoot you. Some believed Americans were too rich to wash their socks and underwear, throwing them away after each use. As a student with a family to support, I spent hours calculating my savings from washing our socks and underwear in America!

Their perceptions of America came from the daily news, which has become our unconscious base for judging other nationalities. We accept our own national news as a routine truth of life, without giving much thought as to its accuracy. However, the same news reported in other countries about the U.S., or vice versa, can result in an entirely different interpretation. This is even more applicable to nations about which we have little or no knowledge. Because of its size and importance, there is more to report from and about the U. S. than other countries. However, generally, ninety percent of the reported news is negative or inaccurate.

Imagine what foreigners' opinions of America would be like if all they knew was from watching television or reading the newspapers whose headlines cover: mass murders, baby snatching, car jackings, drive-by shootings, school kids killing classmates and teachers, or O.J. Simpson's murder trial. The President's scandal with Monica Lewinsky, plus Democratic fund raising from Chinese investors, and so on is a poor representation of America. Watergate, the scandal of the Presidential elections in Florida in 2000, and other news of this kind is downgrading to all Americans. Unfortunately, the burning of churches, the bombing of federal buildings, and the shooting of innocent citizens is all most other people see and know about America. It is no wonder that some foreigners do not have an accurate picture of the United States. People rarely take the time to see both sides before making a judgment.

My wife and I were in France when CNN reported the mass cult suicide in California of 36 young, educated Americans. We had no idea what the French or some other Europeans staying in the hotel might be thinking about Americans. It was difficult for us to answer their innocent and sincere questions in regard to that bizarre incident. The occasional ten percent good news of America's sending a spaceship to Mars, of peacekeeping troops in Bosnia, or of American intellectuals winning the Nobel Prize is wonderful, but it is not nearly enough to offset the negative perceptions about the United States.

My friends and family had similar reasons on which to base their opinions about America. During the 1960's and the Vietnam War, the media coverage produced the worst publicity for America. Witnessing the bombing of innocent school children and hospitals, and hearing reports on the torturing of Vietnamese citizens on Middle Eastern networks definitely did not portray the goodness of America and the ideals of democracy. In the 1990's during Desert Storm and the Gulf War we had a similar situation. Unfortunately, the trend continues today. Americans watch one side of the story, and the rest of the world watches another side.

Most of the residual effects of these conflicts were hidden from the American public, but not from the eyes of the world. I remember Peter Arnett report for CNN from Iraq in regard to fighter bombers hitting the wrong targets. This report was denied by government officials, and the reporter was condemned. Years later, in May 2003, while reporting for MSNBC during the war against Saddam Hussein, this same reporter was fired for saying that American progress in the war was not going according to what government and military officials had predicted.

The comportment of individual citizens of a country can influence us to create impressions that could be applied to the rest of their countrymen. Watching Mikhail Baryshnikov's outstanding performance in a ballet should not make us believe that all Russians are ballerinas, and we probably don't. An Olympic champion gymnast from Rumania should never lead us to think that every Rumanian is a world class gymnast. But as the mind works in mysterious ways, we too often do not hesitate to call all Rumanians, Russians, or Egyptians thieves if someone from that country picked our wallet! Likewise, when anyone from the Middle East plants a bomb, we immediately label all the citizens from that region terrorists. Sadly, this has become more evident since the heinous 9/11 attack on our country.

Tim McVeigh's bombing of the Oklahoma Federal Building, killing 176 people, certainly does not make all Americans murderers and killers in any way. Nor for the same reason is it fair to call an entire ethnic group a name that applies only to a few individuals. We cannot call all Germans Nazis, and we should not label all Moslems as terrorists. The only true way of knowing other nationalities is by traveling to their country, living amongst them, and getting to know them up close and in person. After all, first and foremost, we are human beings, citizens of the world, regardless of differences in place of birth, religion, language, and beliefs.

This reminds me of an incident I had with one of my professors at the University of Northern Colorado. In his class, Building Athletic Fields and Facilities, he asked me if we had any buildings in Iran, assuming that we lived in tents. His ignorance was so astonishing and insulting that I had to say, "Sir, I would rather not answer you," thinking if I opened my big mouth I would be in trouble. My response must have embarrassed him enough to do a little research in which he learned how intricate and delicate is the art of Iran and how advanced the Persian civilization was. He apologized to me a week later, saying he had never seen such beautifully ornate buildings and architectural designs!

This kind of ignorance boggles my mind but I have even more serious difficulties dealing with politicians who make policies based on who pays them more or what kind of financial advantages they may receive. In recent history, China and Russia have violated more human rights than any others; yet, we look the other way because American investors, meaning the rich, are profiting from the low wages paid to their workers, and politicians are collecting their election money.

Today, Iran and other nations are on our black list because they haven't paid a dime to satisfy U.S. politicians. In the past, our politicians accepted and embraced the Shah, because he bought them all. Listening to Newt Gingrich speak about Iran once made me sick to my stomach. He was so ignorant about Iran's history and citizens, that he was shocking. I think that a person of his public stature and influence should be better informed about the country he is criticizing. It would help to take courses in cultural differences, before he knocks another nation.

The lack of knowledge, ignorance, and the subsequent breakdown in communication and understanding reminds me of a funny, cultural incident I had with an American couple in Tehran.

I was driving with three of my best friends for a weekend

getaway to the Caspian Sea, a favorite vacation spot. Ten kilometers outside of Tehran I saw a huge crowd gathered around an accident involving a car and taxi. It is quite typical for people in the region, out of curiosity, to gather around any such incident. This time they had a better incentive—a petite blond in a miniskirt. I stopped and asked my buddies to allow me a minute to find out if I could help, which I always did as part of my nature. They didn't mind.

At the scene there was a policeman, a couple of foreigners, and a taxi driver "drunk as a skunk." The male, who looked like the Marlboro man, was yelling in English nonstop. His cute blond companion seemed very frightened, either from the crowd or the accident, because she was shaking and crying. The policeman and taxi driver, not understanding a word of English, were responding to the man in Farsi. All were shouting at each other without knowing what the other person was saying.

I offered to help by translating. The "Marlboro man" replied, "My God there is someone in this shit hole who can speak the language of human beings instead of this mumbo jumbo." His attitude upset me so much that I turned around to go back to my car. The distraught young woman, choking from her crying, begged me to come back. She said, "We need your help desperately. My husband, Bob, is so angry that he has lost his manners. Please don't let him discourage you. We would appreciate any help you can give us. My name is Kathy; we are Americans working in Tehran."

I learned from the policeman that the couple was traveling north in their own lane. The drunk taxi driver, going south, swerved across the median and hit them head on. Fortunately, no one was hurt. But, he wanted the "Marlboro" man to pay his fine! Thinking that all Americans are rich, the policeman also assumed he had his chance to make some extra money. He had his pad and paper ready, pretending to write a ticket, taking his time, hoping to settle for agreeable cash up front. Kathy, nervous about being placed in an awkward situation and clueless as to what was going to happen, couldn't let go of my arm. She knew they were in trouble in violating their contract by driving in Iran, because of their limited insurance liabilities.

Typically people in the Middle East in a heated discussion all talk at the same time. Bob, the Marlboro man, with his insulting attitude and loud boisterous voice, was acting worse. My job as translator became a very difficult task. I knew I was in a touchy situation as I had to be quite the diplomat in order to please all parties. To play it safe, the proper protocol was to give the police officer full priority; otherwise, I could have been paying the largest fine! I asked Bob to calm down and give me a chance to settle things for them. I told him I was experienced in negotiations and knew how to get things done in the proper way in that country with government officials. The police officer was playing it cool, taking his time.

Bob did not shut up for a second to listen to my advice. Instead, he wanted me to ask the stupid policeman, "What is his f.....'in problem? The taxi driver was the one at fault for being excessively drunk and driving on the wrong side of the road." He demanded that the policeman make the taxi driver pay for damage to his car. Contrary to what he expected to hear, the officer stated, "Why does this idiot think the taxi driver is at fault? How can he blame him? The poor man is drunk!" Then, he asked me to translate to "idiot" Bob that it was his fault. He was the "guilty one," not watching for drunk drivers on the road, and should pay for the damages to the taxi, plus a fine for not being a defensive driver.

Imagine my position! It was impossible to explain this logic to a hotheaded big fellow, let alone call him "idiot." In his anger, he grabbed me by my shirt collar and tried to choke me to take out his frustrations. I was the innocent passerby who was only trying to help, not expecting a childish attack. The blond bombshell wife, still crying hysterically, tried to calm Bob down while asking me to ignore him. She begged me not to leave. "I will do anything, if you just get us out of this mess. You name your price and I will pay it," she said. Obviously, she knew about corruption and *roshveh*!

But Bob made me so angry that I warned him to take his hands off me or I would leave. Having no other alternative, the Marlboro man let go of my shirt. With his improper behavior, the policeman stated: "Besides a large fine, I have to take them to the police station for aggravated assault on an innocent citizen." His remark truly frightened me. Bob was so naive, not knowing what could happen to him and his wife if they were taken to a police station in Iran. I was not going to have this on my conscious, knowing that if they went into that corrupt police station, Kathy's life would never be the same. The chance of her being raped by everyone in the station was undeniable.

I told the two Americans that they were in a country where bargaining could be the solution, not logic. I would negotiate with the policeman to agree to the lowest possible amount if Bob would be quiet, leave me alone, stay out of my way, and not make things worse with his temper. I emphasized that if they wanted to resolve the problem without any further complications he would have to let me negotiate for them; otherwise, they could be in a more complicated legal mess than they could handle.

He apologized, realizing he had no other choice. Still mistrusting me, he asked how much I would be getting out of the deal. With that insult, I started walking to my car. Kathy ran after me, trying to hug me and hang onto me to prevent my departure. Her unacceptable public behavior, groping a man in the street in front of other people, in a Moslem country, shocked the heck out of the crowd! My friends, watching from a distance, didn't know what in the world was happening. The all-male Moslem crowd went wild. I'll never forget their puzzled faces. She persuaded me to go back. Within thirty minutes I settled everything with $50 for the policeman, and without a ticket or an official report. The policeman originally wanted $300 equally split between the taxi driver and himself.

After all I did for Bob, instead of thanking me, he asked if I would honestly tell him how much I pocketed out of that deal.

107

His ridiculous out-of-line remark made me realize the meaning of "Ugly American." His wife was humiliated in front of me. I assumed they must have had problems together before, but this was the final straw that broke the camel's back and she said to Bob, "I am not sitting in the same car with you." Then she heatedly added, "In fact, I don't care if I ever see your face again!"

Crying hysterically, she turned to me and asked if I would give her a ride home. I answered, "We aren't going to Tehran, we are on our way to the Caspian Sea." She looked a bit confused and then said, "Oh, who cares, as long as you take me back to Tehran on your return."

Bob started calling Kathy ugly names, causing her so much embarrassment as to make her walk towards my car without waiting for my answer. My friends didn't know what she was doing, but they had great pleasure opening the door and making space for her in the back seat of the crowded car. In their good natured way, they fought over who was going to sit next to her as she practically had to sit on their laps. After her long, scary, unpleasant day of crying, she had a great time with three good-looking Persian men, each vying for her attention.

My last days in Tehran were the most pleasant ones. I vividly remember a few of those comical incidents. I must have been so thrilled with my exit that none of the sad occasions come to my mind!

Tehran's Mehr Abad Airport looked more exciting on our departure day than on any other trip I had previously taken from there. Friends, relatives, close fans, and well-wishers all were gathered to say their final farewell and wish us good luck in our new venture. I couldn't recognize them all or know their names. I felt the ultimate joy visualizing the bright daylight my grandmother had always talked about.

Although I knew I was so close to saving my family from repression, I could not ignore a nagging fear that still something could go wrong preventing us from getting on our airplane. I knew the SAVAK would not wear uniforms to avoid being recognized, but I still couldn't help myself from looking around to be sure no one was going to stop us from leaving. I kept praying to Allah and had my fingers crossed, hoping nothing would go wrong at the last minute.

Finally, feeling the jet take off made me the most fulfilled man on earth. I had absolutely no intentions of returning and dealing with a corrupt government again. Witnessing my success in getting away gave me a new sense of strength, even though I had a subconscious fear of not being totally free because of the Shah's power in the United States. Instead, I decided to concentrate on one day at a time and that everything would be all right.

In visualizing my family's future, none of the negative factors seemed to matter to me. Then I thought, if there were no way for me to be free, at least my wife and daughter would have infinite life choices. And because of my plans, they wouldn't have to live locked behind closed doors for the rest of their lives. As we flew away from our homeland, the fantastic feeling of achievement made me joyfully thank my wonderful grandmother for teaching me never to give up and to "go for the gold."

Author with the late Shah's brother in Khoramshahr,
Iran at the opening ceremony of the state's first
indoor arena, 1963. The governor, the head of
the Navy, and other officials follow behind.

CONQUERING ENGLISH IN AMERICA

The realization that I was now about to live my dreams was so exciting that it made the sixteen hour flight from Tehran to New York fly by. Because of the time difference when we approached America, it was still daylight which allowed me to see the "final bright daylight" my grandmother had consoled me with when I was young.

I could not wait to be in New York City! But sadly I had to put my enthusiasm on hold because we were not able to clear customs. One of the requirements for entry into the U.S. was proof of good health, i.e., x-rays and medical records. No one had advised me that these important documents should be hand carried, and I had assumed they were for my admission to the university. As a result, I had securely placed them in the bottom of my large suitcase.

My heart sank even further when an airline agent informed me that our three precious suitcases could not be found. I was devastated by the thought that what was left of our entire life's belongings was lost. I was shaking and had a knot in my stomach.

The airline agent calmly and politely asked for my permanent address, which for her, was a routine procedure. But for me, this was all new, and the panic on my face was plain to see. I did not have even a temporary address, let alone a permanent one. Anxious and nervous, I informed the agent that I was not leaving until my suitcases were found and delivered to me. I requested three blankets and said that we would sleep in front of their office. The woman kindly told me that it was not necessary to sleep in the airport because Pan Am would pay for us to stay in a hotel until the suitcases were found and delivered. I breathed a sigh of relief, but unfortunately too soon.

The customs agent appeared in front of us and told us quite simply, and I must say rudely, that we were not going anywhere until he saw our medical records. He would not allow us to move, much less go back to speak with airline personnel regarding the status of our suitcases. Instead, we were quarantined in a small, jail-like room without a window or ventilation. The heat and humidity of New York in July, plus the entire embarrassing episode, made us feel totally humiliated.

My daughter, Sima, was wearing a pretty yellow dress with a bright bow in her gleaming jet black hair. My wife was wearing a stylish blue suit with matching pumps and her best gold jewelry. I had on gray flannel slacks with a blue button-down shirt, tie, and navy blue blazer. Thus, we thought that we made a favorable impression, but to be treated as if we were refugees from a disease-ridden village was a slap in the face. In Tehran, we were of the upper class and carried ourselves with pride and dignity. I felt crestfallen to have arrived in the country of our dreams, only to be treated in such a disgraceful manner.

In Iran, cleanliness is thought to be next to godliness, and people are required to bathe and wash five times a day to pray. So you can imagine the indignation we felt.

We became even more miserable watching two-year old Sima, a typically active child, being forced to sit still in the hot confines of the small room. She began to cry which made Hava and me, tired ourselves, even more distraught.

The three of us sat in that box-like room for six long hours without anything to eat and only warm water from the faucet to drink. The Pan American agents continued to search for our lost suitcases and finally, informed us that our bags had been located in Los Angeles! The customs agent, upon hearing this, at last permitted us to leave without presenting our medical records. How ironic compared to their being so critical six hours prior!

Needless to say, our first impression of America was not something to write home about. Having known Americans as being friendly, helpful, kind, compassionate people, I was taken aback with the harsh treatment displayed by the customs agents.

Our next surprise came when we saw New York City, hardly what I thought it or America would look like. It was rough, and I said to myself, "I hope the rest of the nation is much friendlier than what we observe here."

Even though from a large city like Tehran, in some strange emotional way the fast pace of life in NYC frightened me. Also, I knew that I did not have a return ticket, and I was determined not to *give up* easily. I took solace in knowing that our stay in the Big Apple was only temporary, tenaciously holding on to my belief that America was *"the land of milk and honey"* which I had read and dreamt about for years. I was assuming that Laramie, Wyoming, my university town, would be the paradise I was seeking!

To my utter dismay, it was in New York City when I realized with horror, for the very first time, that I would have some *"big time"* difficulties with the American language. Communicating, specifically with some African-Americans, became a much harder task for me than I had ever anticipated. Even the simple daily greetings became a major struggle to comprehend and answer. Their *rapid-fire* slang was impossible to understand. There was no way that I could translate from American English to British English and then to Farsi. In Iran, we were taught the Queen's English, but with a Persian accent. We also were told that we should use "sir or madam" when addressing a stranger and that calling someone "man" was considered rude.

To share with you the magnitude of my struggle in learning American English, from this point forward I shall *italicize* the unfamiliar American slangs which gave me such a hard time. For the average American speaker, many of them do not need explanations. However, you may begin to realize the enormity of confusion the expressions and slangs create in a foreigner's mind, especially with the frequency and the different accents with which they are said.

For example, when a New Yorker approached me and asked, *"What's cooking, man?,"* I had no idea what he meant. I

113

had to ask for a bit of clarification, "Pardon me, sir, who is cooking what?" Similarly, I had a difficult time answering many other questions, such as, "*How's it going, dude*?", "*What's shaking, bro*?" and "*What's up, doc*?" It took time to decipher what was meant by, "Can you *spare me some change, pal*?" or "*Hey hunk, you've got a dime*?" As I did not know the meaning of *hunk* or *dime,* how was I supposed to understand what was wanted of me?

Once someone asked me, "How do you like the *Big Apple?*" obviously meaning NYC. I told him "I love apples; they are good for your health!" None of these expressions made any sense to me then and created great confusion in my mind. It was a very long time before I dared to answer people without hesitating about what they might be saying.

My first major communication problem occurred after settling in a hotel, courtesy of Pan American Airlines, minus our suitcases. I was so anxious to go for a walk downtown that even after sixteen hours of travel, being detained for six hours, and the additional time needed at the hotel, didn't *dampen* my enthusiasm. All my wife wanted to do was take a shower, and she asked me while I was exploring the city if I would buy her a new bra to change into. Without thinking of the English word for it, I took off telling her, " No problem, I would be glad to."

Can you imagine what it would be like walking into a store in Manhattan without knowing the English word for bra? As I wandered about looking lost and perplexed, a sales girl asked me, "Can I help you?" I said, "Yes, please;" however, my dilemma was not knowing how to ask for what I wanted. I could not show her mine, since I didn't wear one! And certainly, out of good manners, I could not touch hers to show her what I needed. Therefore, our conversation became quite intriguing as she listened to my stilted English and vain attempt at communication. She kept shaking her head up and down, making me think she understood what I was looking for. In her mind, she might have even assumed that I was making compliments or *coming on to her*.

Pointing to her breast, she wanted to know if I liked women with large breasts. I thought she was referring to the size of bra I needed to buy. While she expected me to smile and say yes, I said, "Oh no, that is too big." She became extremely angry with me and acted like she wanted to throw me out. I rushed out of the store, totally confused, without having the slightest idea of what I had done wrong to upset this nice lady. After all, she was the one who had come to me volunteering her help.

All the way back to the hotel, my mind was so twisted that I couldn't think straight. To complicate matters, I had to deal with a mugger. Of course, naive me didn't realize it at the time, as I had no prior experience with mugging. In Tehran, and in many big European cities, I had seen professional pickpockets. They were very well trained, worked in teams, and performed as quickly as magicians. In a split second your jewelry, wallet, and money were taken without your feeling a thing. Either because of stricter laws or having rather more skillful thieves, few robbers in those countries would hold a gun or knife to a person's throat and force them to hand over their cash and valuables.

The mugger called to me; "*Hey man*, bring your *white ass up here.*" With my limited vocabulary "*ass*" meant donkey, and I did not have a white donkey. Further more, he was standing next to me not above me, so how could I go "*up*" to him. I looked behind me, just to be sure that someone else's donkey wasn't there. I told him, "I don't have a white ass; you must be mistaken." Then sympathetically I asked him if he had lost his white ass. That made him angry and he shouted, "Don't *jive my ass*, man, *my ass is black.*" Not knowing what he was talking about, I thought I was losing my mind or my eyesight, as I could not see a "black donkey" anywhere around either.

By then he was really mad. He yelled: "Don't *mess with me*; I am a mother f...'er! Quit being a f...'in *wise ass* you *dumb shit*, just give me your *dough*!" Then he pulled out a big knife and shouted: "I'll *gut* your *f... 'in throat*!" I knew the meaning of "cut" but had no idea what the word "gut" meant. Needless to say, his throwing in such words as "f...." with throat really *threw me off*. If you think I was totally *messed up* before, try to imagine my reaction when primal fear was added to the equation. *For the life of me*, I could not figure out what he wanted. How could a donkey be "wise" or "shit" be intelligent? The "f..." word was an unrelated vulgarity that I would never have learned in proper British English in school. How is it possible to *jive* a donkey, and of course I didn't know what *jiving* meant. And, what did *"dough"* have to do with any of this? Did he think that I was a baker?

My years of learning English in high school and college were of no help in trying to understand him. The situation was getting more and more intense which made me realize that I had better get out of it as soon as possible. I thought the only way for me to escape the situation was to *give him a knee*, and run. Fortunately, I was a fast sprinter and in good shape. *Later on*, I found out how lucky I was to act on impulse; otherwise, I'm sure that I would have been robbed *big time*, as I had a large amount of cash on me. Hearing the word "ass" in different contexts in later years, often reminded me of my dreadful experience, especially when I had to figure out the meanings of expressions like: *ass hole, pompous ass, hard ass, fat ass, dumb ass, jack ass, tight ass*, and a lot more unsavory references.

Another adventure was trying to order from a restaurant menu. There were several occasions with which I had a *tough time*. For example, I couldn't imagine what a *hot dog* was. I knew the meaning of "hot" and "dog", but I couldn't believe my eyes when I saw on the menu *hot dog* and wondered how Americans could eat *hot dogs*. My curiosity was *killing* me. At that time a hot dog only cost about 35 cents, but it still took me seven days *to muster enough courage* to order one. I had no real desire to eat it. First, I had to smell it, to know if I would even *go any further*. Acting like a *nerd*, I looked around to be sure that no one was watching me. Then I carefully opened the bun to see what this popular food looked like. Immediately, I closed it and left it on my plate. The waitress noticed that I had not touched my meal. She approached me and asked if there was anything wrong with my order. I was embarrassed to answer; so, I said no, nothing is wrong. She was too nice and kept insisting that she would be glad to *get me* something else with no charge. She stood over me politely waiting for my reply, and I felt awkward. I quietly whispered to her that, "I don't want this part of the dog. "

My next adventure in ordering a meal was in a cafeteria. I thought it was best to keep a sharp eye and close ear on the two men in front of me. If I liked what they ordered, I would repeat what they said. They asked for eggs and that seemed okay to me. I liked eggs. The problem came, however, when the server asked the men, "How would you like your eggs?" They said, "*Over easy.*" When I saw the soft, oozy, floppy eggs, which wasn't to my liking, I decided to say the opposite. I ordered mine, "*Under difficult.*" If they had said "soft", I could have ordered mine "hard," but the only opposite word I knew for "easy" was "difficult." The server thought I was being a *smart ass*. I honestly did not know how many different ways eggs could be prepared, only learning later: *sunny side up, medium, scrambled, busted, poached,* and so on. Boy, did I get difficult eggs that day!

Everything in NYC seemed new but fascinating to me. One day, while I was looking at cameras in a store window, as photography was one of my favorite hobbies, a young male standing a few shops away kept making gestures. I didn't know if he wanted me or someone in the store, so I looked around, but I didn't see anyone else. He kept hissing and pointing in a direction away from the window, while watching both sides of the street to see who else was there. Apparently, he wanted to be sure no *cops* were in the area. Hesitantly, I went toward him trying to discern what he was trying frantically to tell me. He had a ring in one hand and a jewelry box in the other, and he asked me if I wanted a "big bargain." Not knowing what the word "bargain" meant, and as I thought he was referring to the ring, I said, "That isn't a big bargain, it is a small ring." He replied, "I am telling you, man, this is a real big bargain." To avoid any argument, I told him, "Whatever you say, if you think this is a bargain instead of a ring, *so be it*." He continued, "You give me 65 *bucks*, I'll let you have this *awesome deal* that is worth a *grand*!" I was totally confused, not knowing what to say or do in response to any of his comments. To me b-u-c-k-s sounded exactly the same as b-o-x. I couldn't comprehend how was he expecting me to give him 65 boxes if I didn't even know the sizes he needed? I forced myself to be quiet to think and make sense out of what he was saying. I had no idea what he meant by *a grand* either. I assumed he needed a giant size box for some strange reason!

Then he asked, how about 50 *bucks*? I kept telling him, "I don't have any boxes, you should go and ask at some of the stores; they must have plenty of them." He kept rambling, "*Come on man, give me a break; 35 bucks* and *you got it*." I was puzzled by his persistent request for "boxes" from me and did not appreciate his thinking that *I've got* the boxes but am unwilling to give them to him. His continual reduction of the number of boxes kept adding to my confusion. I shook my head and told him he was asking for boxes from the wrong person.

He placed the ring in the box and then took a woman's ring out, again looking both ways cautiously. Then he started asking me if I had a *chick*. I replied, "Yes, I have two," while touching the sides of my face. He *sort of* became angry with me, thinking I was making fun of him. Then disgustedly in a heated voice said, "I mean *chicken, man, chicken*!" He continued: "If you *wanna score* with your *chick* tonight, this is it, this is *the way to score*." This bizarre conversation made me assume that he thought I was a farmer. I just could not figure out how anyone could "score" with a chicken. I wondered what kind of game American men played with chickens? To be polite and avoid any arguments with him I said, "Sir, I would not mind going to a few stores to find boxes for you but you must tell me the sizes you need. For that, I will not take a ring from you for payment." By then, he *gave up* on selling me a ring and left, *cussing*. Luckily for me, I did not understand a word of what he was saying. I would have been happy with a single thank you, instead of all that "foreign" jargon he spouted off at me.

I had to sit down for awhile on the edge of a concrete flower box just to *pull myself together*. I'm not quite sure who I was feeling sorry for, the man with the rings or myself for my inability to understand his request. For a long time, wherever I went, the ring and chicken conversation kept coming to my mind. Many nights I dreamed about the young man, thinking how sad and poor his life must have been that he had to trade jewelry for boxes. I felt guilty for not having been able to help him.

Because of various similar incidents, I realized that sheer determination to make it in my new country might not be enough to guarantee me of success. I was anxious and scared, thinking it was not going to be easy to survive in my new country.

With a *knot in the pit of my stomach*, I sat down on a park bench to *catch my breath*. Fortuitously, this happened to be one of life's luckiest moments for me. I looked up to see a very close friend of mine from Iran, standing there staring at me. What a surprise! Neither one of us expected to see one another in NYC. There was a long silence before we spoke a word. I said his name, "Majid?" as he shouted, "Parviz!" and joyfully we embraced each other. Jumping up and down with excitement like two little kids, both of us asked at the same time, "What are you doing here?" I told him about my coaching position in Wyoming and our subsequent layover in New York because of lost luggage, and that we were leaving the next day for Wyoming. He insisted that we must stay longer.

He said he had a nice apartment in Manhattan and wanted me to meet his wife and daughter. He explained how he came to NYC several years ago as a visitor, met a lovely Iranian girl, Juliet, who was an American resident, fell in love, married, and now lived and worked in New York.

119

Majid was a true Iranian who would not take no for an answer, and as with all Persians, he would not hesitate to share whatever he had with his friends and family. He accompanied me to our hotel, helped my wife pack, then took us to his place, where we stayed for two weeks. Majid and Juliet were absolutely the most gracious host and hostess, and because of them, I witnessed another side of NYC which I had heretofore not experienced.

To fulfill a lifelong dream, my very first request for sightseeing was the Statue of Liberty, which Majid and Juliet took us to visit the next day. Bedloe's or Liberty Island was more exciting than I had imagined, and we had a gorgeous day to make the visit even more memorable.

Fascinated with the statue, I slipped away for ten minutes, just contemplating and thanking Allah and the Lady for helping me get there. I felt as if I had won the Olympic gold medal by awarding freedom to myself and my family. After a lifetime of hardship, struggle, and starvation, I felt I was on top of a victory stand on a podium. I did not want anyone to see me crying for joy. When Majid found me he could not avoid *chewing me out* for being careless and *wandering away* from the group. I apologized and promised him not to do it again.

At the time, I did not understand why he was so angry or why he and Juliet had been staying so close to us and watching over every movement. They, however, knew the dangers that life in New York could bring to ingenuous newcomers. It seemed rather awkward at the time, but I sincerely appreciated it later and thanked them both profusely.

Having them explain and describe everything in detail was the best training we could have received to survive. They were an enormous help, and I am forever grateful. Majid and his family moved to San Francisco a few years later, and unfortunately I lost contact with them.

In later years, my brother, wrote a song upon seeing the Statue of Liberty which in turn inspired me to write this poem.

THE LADY

When my eyes first met the lady's,
I was far away from home.
I had left my country, friends, and family,
for America, without a home.
I knew the road I would travel
would be a tough and lonely one,
but I heard the lady
call to me as her "newest son."
Her arms soon embraced me,
and showed her welcome plain.
She knew I was worried, but
she showed me what I would gain.
A new home called America,
where each man can be free
to seek opportunities, to be the best he can be.
She gave me the inspiration that I needed,
and made me happy about the ideas that I had seeded.
I felt very happy for my daughter and my wife
Knowing that they would not have to live a dictated life.
With joy I thanked God, cried, and prayed
Then, from the bottom of my heart I said
America, your freedom is all that I need;
America, America, my eternal home indeed.

With my friend's knowledgeable and invaluable guidance, NYC became exciting. Even though at times the city was still frightening, it did not affect my enormous delight in touring the *Big Apple*.

Two days later I was able to get away by myself for a few hours. Once again I rushed to Bedloe's Island to visit The Lady. After crying awhile, I thanked her and God once again for helping us to escape from Iran and granting my family and me freedom which every individual deserves to have. I prayed and begged God to grant me enough strength to continue the uphill battle to survive in America and to give my family a chance to live free, no matter what might happen to me.

My struggle to learn English proficiently has been a never-ending process. Even now, more than three and a half decades later, with all the knowledge and extensive vocabulary I have gained, I am not quite sure if I can truly say that *I've got it*, nor am I totally comfortable with the language. Every day, I learn new words and expressions. Believe me, the struggle *goes on*.

Walking around my friend's apartment building provided me another unique experience. A pretty, young blond girl of about 18 or 19 was *hanging out* there, often greeting and talking to people in front of the apartment or in the lobby. She was pleasant enough and very approachable, so for the first few days I actually looked forward to seeing and exchanging common greetings with her to *polish* my English. Our conversations soon became so confusing that I tried on some occasions to avoid communicating with her.

The weirdest conversation with that young girl revolved around my teaching her to say my name correctly. Regardless of how many times I pronounced and spelled it for her, she could not say it. She kept calling me *stud*, which I understood and heard as similar to "Steve" and did not like. On one occasion, she asked me when I was going to *ditch* the *old lady* so she could *show me a good time*. It puzzled me thinking, which *"old lady"* had she seen me with? I was *going nuts* trying to remember when in New York I had an old lady with me? It seemed so cruel to talk about "ditching" an old lady. And then, how can a person "show" someone a good time? I thought she probably meant having a good time, but I was not quite sure. Each day she became more aggressive, causing me to be further *messed up* in my sincere efforts to understand her or give the right answer to her questions. At times today, I recall her exact words which now make me laugh. This naturally gives others around me, who do not know what I am *giggling about*, a rather odd feeling. Often I have noticed that they wonder what *I'm up to*. Those particular conversations were not funny at the time, as they gave me serious discomfort and often made me feel foolish. But now, they seem comical.

One of our *off the wall* conversations went like this: "Hey *stud*, how about a *quickie*, twenty *bucks*, with me and you can *have your way. Everything goes* for fifty *bucks*." I had no idea what she wanted me to say in response to *"everything can go for fifty box,"* and indeed where would they be going. Adding more confusion, she said, "I am so *good in bed* that I can make you sing *hallelujah*." How can a person be "good" or "bad" in bed? For me, a bed was a place to sleep. I didn't know the song "hallelujah," and how was a Moslem suppose to sing it? "Come on, man," she told me one day, "I *wanna get it on with you*. What are you waiting for, Christmas?" What did Christmas have to do with any of our conversations in July? How can a person *get it "on"* or *"off"* with others?

Finally the young girl told me, "I can see that you are a *chicken shit* and don't have the *guts* to *ditch* your *old lady*. I'm disappointed in you. I know who *wears the pants in your house*; it sure isn't you."

Quickie and her other unfamiliar proposals were not the only *words throwing me off balance*. It was figuring out the *drift* of her entire conversation. To give myself a chance to ask Majid to explain to me how I could help that poor girl, I said, "Thanks, that was very nice of you to give me your *best deal*. Let me see what we can do about it. I will get back with you *in a jiffy*."

Talking about this incident with my friend became the funniest topic at their dinner table. They recognized the girl, a young prostitute, who did not live in the building but often came to visit a friend. Neither Majid or Juliet made fun of me for asking those stupid questions, but my wife was disgusted with me and blamed me for asking the young girl about her services and fees. Hava's true personality seemed to be surfacing once more, but I dealt with it as always, by ignoring her criticism. Her accusations caused my friends to laugh even harder because they realized that she didn't trust me, but they knew me to be a better person than that. For the rest of our stay there, I had to hide from that girl to avoid more embarrassment.

This chapter by itself could be a lengthy book if I tried to relate all my experiences in learning English. But, I would like to move on to my next destination, Laramie, Wyoming.

I found only two choices to take my family from New York City to Laramie. One was a flight from NYC to Denver, Colorado, and then hoping to find some sort of ground transportation to Laramie. The thought of losing our luggage again was too painful. Our remaining and hopefully less problematic option was to take the Greyhound Bus to Laramie, which is what we did. I initially thought it would be exciting to see the rest of America this way. Need I say more?

What with our two year old daughter, the great distance, waiting in bus stations, stopping at truck stops, the complication of changing buses, this option ended up to be *quite an ordeal*. I saw more farms and corn fields in one trip than I have seen in my entire life. The only redeeming thing was that we made it to Laramie without a major problem. However, our cross country journey was nothing compared to the despair I felt upon entering Laramie!

What a shock! The transition from having spent three weeks in NYC, one of the most populated, cosmopolitan cities of the world to the isolated, quiet, ranch town of Laramie, was going to necessitate an enormous adjustment. The positive side was that the people in Wyoming helped us in many ways. They were so friendly and helpful that I wondered if I had entered a different country. I must say, however, that the town and its environment created a huge cultural and emotional shock. This would take some time getting used to!

I gradually fell in love with Laramie, seeing and accepting it as our first home in our new country. I must express how thankful I am to the many gracious people there who took my family and me under their protection and made us feel more comfortable in our new setting. Nonetheless, I must confess that I could have picked a warmer, larger town for my first home. Laramie is windy and cold.

I was accepted at other universities, but the University of Wyoming had offered me a position and job first, so I had *grabbed* it. Also, I didn't know the difference between individual states in America. I had few literary resources in Iran, and without the vast knowledge that internet provides today to make better choices. It was difficult for me to analyze the differences between Laramie, Wyoming, or Denver, Colorado or Dayton, Ohio.

All I knew was that I was thrilled to come to America. After seven years of waiting, I was not going to let the flat, mundane landscape or bad weather bother me. Three years later when I moved to Colorado, I couldn't believe the majesty of the Rocky Mountains, and I finally started to thaw out. What a difference a relatively small distance can make!

Standing outside the Laramie bus station, with our three suitcases, my daughter, an Iranian wife who hated America and who could not speak a word of English, forced me into a reality check. I was sick to my stomach not knowing what to do next. I had no idea where we were supposed to go from the bus station. Was there a taxi service in such a small town, and if so, how do I get one? And should I be so lucky to find a taxi, where would I ask the driver to take us?

It suddenly felt like the *whole world was on my shoulders*. I went to the back of the building and there alone, so that my wife and daughter would not see my tears and fear, started crying. I also started to pray. I had faith in God that he would help me through this *tough time,* as he had so many times in the past.

After sobbing alone, in my depressed state, it occurred to me that the head of the university athletic department who hired me would be the best source for assistance. That was the best decision I could have made. His name was Ray Jacoby, and he was the most wonderful man I have ever met. He helped me more than could be imagined, in spite of my inability to communicate accurately.

I gathered my family and we finally found a cabdriver who drove us to the campus and to his office. Because of his winning football team, there was hardly anyone in town who did not know Ray Jacoby. As soon as I introduced myself, he said with excitement: *"By golly,* I see with all of your *credentials,* you are a *hell* of a coach and a *peach of a guy!"*

His greeting totally *threw me off.*

He spoke too fast and I was stuck on the meaning of " by golly" and "credentials." I also didn't understand why he associated me with the word "hell." I felt good that I knew what a "peach" was, but what it had to do with me or a guy just left me *dumbfounded.* In short, it was impossible for me to reply. I asked him, "Pardon me, sir, are you talking to me?"

Mr. Jacoby suddenly realized he was speaking too fast and using words that I did not know. Laughing, he apologized and spoke more slowly. He shook my hand and said, "Oh, don't worry, everything is *going to be cool."* Then he added, "You come to Red," pointing to himself, "anytime when other people cannot understand you" I was embarrassed to ask him any questions, as he was trying his best to help me. Of course, calling himself the color "red" presented its own problem. I wondered since he had so much trouble understanding me, how he expected to help others to understand what I was trying to say.

Feeling sorry for me, he arranged for us to move into a

university guest house. He then called Keith, another coach who became a good friend, to take us there. Keith later helped me with many other things, including finding a place to rent.

When I started coaching for *Red*, a number of our everyday conversations were quite bewildering to me. His referring to college mascots as *tigers, rams, buffaloes, eagles,* and other animals with which I was not familiar *messed me up good,* or shall I say *messed me up real bad?* How *odd* that in English we use "good" and "bad" interchangeably even though they are opposites.

Ray would try to *pump me up* before a game; thus, he would slap me on the back and say, *"Hey,* coach, *go get them bighorns,"* which unfortunately did not mean *squat* to me. It was not easy to ask him for clarification and I did not know to whom to turn for a translation. Needless to say, the dictionary did not help me to connect "animals" to universities. So there I was perplexed and frustrated once again.

When Ray asked: "Coach, *do you have your ducks in a row?"* I replied, "What gave you the idea that I was going hunting?" He laughed and said: *"Boy!* you've got a good sense of humor." While he was laughing he called me, *"Foozi"* (which in Persian is a female name and to which I took offense) . Regardless of how many times I spelled and pronounced my name for him, as nice and kind as he was, Ray simply could not *get it right* and kept calling me *Foozi.*

One day he said, *"Foozi,* you *tickle me to death."* I responded to him, " Sir, I didn't touch you." Instead of agreeing with me he laughed harder and accused me of *choking him to death.* Since I had such respect for him I decided to *let it go.*

Then he said to me, "You make me *laugh my heart out.* I did not think that statement was quite flattering either. I apologized for "hurting his health" still without knowing what I was doing wrong. He laughed so hard that it seemed like he was really choking. I ran to his secretary for help but she just ignored me and laughingly said, "Oh, don't worry, he's all right. *Red* tells me you make him *split a gut,* and he is always getting

127

a *kick out of you.*

With her apparent accusation of my "kicking" and "splitting" Ray's *gut,* I became angry and left the office. When I think about it she also confused me as to why everyone called Ray, *Red.* As much as I adored Mr. Jacoby, I tried to avoid conversations with him, especially after he said, *"Foozi, you crack me up."*

On one occasion, after winning a very important game, he slapped me on the *butt,* which just wasn't done in Iran. We patted the athletes *on their heads* instead of *their behinds.* Then he told the track coach, "I love *Foozi; he is after my heart.* Did you hear that he *beat the pants off them Falcons!"* His choice of words, calling me by a girl's name, and touching my butt embarrassed me instead of making me proud. He saw the puzzled expression on my face and said, " Come coach, let me *buy ya a cup of coffee."*

I thought he's taking me to a coffee shop. But, no, he just poured me coffee in his office without *buying* a thing. I felt that I shouldn't say a word, but I had many lingering questions in my mind.

In spite of our differences linguistically, during the three seasons which I coached at the University of Wyoming, Mr. Jacoby proved to be the most appreciative of my ability and dedication.

He rewarded me financially much more than my contract called for by paying me beyond what I had expected. He was the most exceptional boss I ever worked for. His winsome personality and generous support made me forget about the many arduous times I had understanding him in our conversations.

Before our first game he told me, "Coach, *break a leg,*" a normal good luck wish in America but unfamiliar to me. I didn't know if he wanted our team to break the leg of one of the opponents by playing rough, or if he was hoping one of our boys would break a leg. I replied quickly, "No sir, I hope no one breaks a leg."

The day before our game against the Air Force Academy, Mr. Jacoby made a special effort to call and tell me, *"Get them Falcons, tiger."* Without knowing what he meant and out of admiration for him, I replied, "Yes, sir, you can be sure of that," and I hung up.

Although I made Ray Jacoby uncomfortable at times with my ignorance of American slang, I must have impressed him with my coaching ability, because he told me that he did not want me to transfer to any other university. However, should I decide to leave, if I needed a recommendation, I should tell them to call *Red*, collect! His kind, sincere words were and have always been, my best coaching reward.

Providentially, Ray introduced me to a graduate student named Keith McCoy, who was studying for his doctoral exam. Keith insisted that I call on him for any of my important family needs. As a result, he took my family shopping and expressed that the best gift I gave him in turn was making him laugh. He said, "I was his only entertainment while he *studied like a dog.*" I dared not ask him how a dog can study! Beyond his terrific personality, I sincerely believe that he above all others understood how difficult the simplest tasks were for someone living in a new country.

Keith was especially helpful to us with grocery shopping, which alone proved to be a major undertaking. Not being familiar with the large variety of merchandise on the grocery shelves made it very difficult to buy the right items. Without Keith, we wasted more money buying things we could not use or return. When we needed a can of tuna fish, we would take the first one labeled "tuna" in large print, without reading the additional small print. I did not realize how many choices there were in America, some of which we did not like at all. For example, there was Whole Milk, Skim Milk, Low Fat Milk, 1% Milk, etc. Also, I didn't know that people could return or exchange items, another difference between our two countries.

Choices in the U.S. reminds me of a funny experience I had in Tehran with two American friends, Dr. Burgess and his wife,

Linda. I walked into a restaurant and found them totally frustrated in their efforts to order their food. Dr. Burgess wanted fresh milk with his meal and Linda wished to have low fat milk. The waiters, manager, and restaurant owner, in an effort to satisfy their respected guests had asked every person in the room to help translate the items the couple desired. Because there is only one kind of milk known to everyone, the staff assumed what the Americans wanted was a specific milk product. Therefore, they brought to their table everything they could think of that was made from milk and still couldn't satisfy them. The moment Linda and Wayne saw me walk into the restaurant they were relieved to have me translate and end the confusion. Instead, I had to explain to them the nonexistence of so many selections in Iran. This embarrassed them and they apologized to the staff for their ignorance. Then everyone in the restaurant began laughing. The owner was so relieved that he gave me my meal "*on the house.*"

One day, while returning home from grocery shopping with Keith, he suddenly got upset with himself and started hitting the steering wheel and said *son of a gun*! He slowed down, made a U turn and mumbled a few more words, which I did not understand. He said, "Sorry, Parviz, my wife wanted some *f... 'in potatoes* and I forgot to buy them; we have to go back." I was taken aback by his change of mood and language. I just stared at him. He apologized and said, "I'm sorry, were you in a hurry to get home?" I replied, "No, Keith, I am not, please don't turn around. But I would love to know *what kind of potatoes* you're buying and *who is a son of a gun*?"

His wife, Donna, was yet another kind and helpful person, who assisted us in many ways. She brought newspapers home with rental ads and helped make telephone calls for us. I tried doing it myself at first, but my lack of English, made speaking on the phone a little complicated. When the gentleman at the other end said, "Sorry, we have *no vacancy*," I did not understand what *vacancy* meant. I said to him, "Who asked for *vacancy*? I was calling about the house you had advertised for rent." The man thought I was *being cute*, asking me, "Are you *kidding me*?" This time, not knowing who "kidding" was, I replied, " No, I'm Parviz Emamian." The poor guy realized how *off base* I was and explained slowly, "Sorry, sir, we had an apartment but rented it yesterday to someone else." His simple answer, using words familiar to me, made it easy for me to understand.

Once, while I was using the urinal in a campus restroom a very obese man walked in and stood next to me without using the facility. His presence made me nervous. I turned to see what he wanted when he casually asked, "Hey *honkie*, what you *got for a hit* ?" I thought he was making fun of my "head," misunderstanding the word "hit." Feeling very uncomfortable next to him, I ran out of the restroom without finishing my job with my pants zipped only half way.

At another time, Keith and I were walking to the student center to have a cup of coffee when we saw the custodian mopping the floor in the hallway. Keith asked, "*How's it going*, Bill?" He answered, "I'm *still kicking*, Keith." That exchange *got to me* and *got to me good*. Their conversation did not made sense. I asked Keith, "Did Bill say he was kicking? What was he kicking? He didn't have a ball; he was not *kicking the bucket*; there was nothing else around to kick."

Laughing hysterically Keith said, "Parviz, you are *so cool*, you *crack me up* and you make me *laugh my heart out*." That didn't set well with me either. I mistook his calling me "cool" as being cold! Unaware of the different terminology, I politely apologized for "cracking him up and hurting his heart." I promised to be more careful, even though I didn't know what I was supposed to be careful about. He never answered my question about the "kicking," because he could not stop laughing long enough to *fill me in*.

While having coffee in the cafeteria, Keith pointed out a gorgeous, petite blond, telling me, "I *dig* this girl." It was hard for me to figure out how a man can "dig" a girl. I told myself, *never you mind*, maybe it is an expression for sexual relations in

America and she might be his mistress, a possibility which is not unusual in foreign countries. I forced myself to keep my *trap shut* so he would not think I was stupid by asking too many questions. I kept silent for a while, listening to a song on the intercom, when he exclaimed, "Oh, Parviz, I *dig this record.*" Then, thinking about "digging" and visualizing the depth of a record made me so *mixed up* that I had to ask him, "How can you " dig a record" where there's no place to dig?" He almost *fell out of his chair*, laughing hysterically and looking at my puzzled face. Then he explained that *digging* is another way of expressing *enjoying* or *liking* something.

My first week in graduate school was very exciting, but at the same time made me very nervous and anxious. In addition to the teaching and coaching assignments, I was registered for a full study load. I had no idea what it would be like nor how to prepare myself for classes. The first day each instructor walked into class, introduced himself or herself, and then asked us to do the same. For homework, we were required to read the first two or three chapters of each textbook and be ready to discuss them at our next meeting. I was supposed to read fourteen chapters that week!

When we studied English as a second language in Iran, we had one textbook a year, which we hardly ever finished. And to my dismay, English as a second language was not offered that semester at the university. I was *on my own!*

Filled with anxiety, I set aside the entire weekend to complete my reading assignments. I began Saturday at 9 a.m. and read until midnight with only two short breaks for lunch and dinner. I used my English/Persian and Persian/English dictionaries for every line read but could not make sense of most paragraphs. Finding the meaning for individual words from the dictionary did not help me to understand fully the meaning of the sentences. By midnight, I had only finished one chapter but did not understand any of it

This probably is true in dealing with any second language; learning English is not an exception. However, the influence of

132

Latin added to slang certainly made it more difficult for me. Some words used in reverse order gave me the hardest time, for example, *pretty awful* and *awful pretty*. I knew the meaning of each word individually, but just could not understand how *awful* could be *pretty* or how *pretty* could be used with *awful*. Certain words like *tough* and *shit* were very hard to figure out. *Tough luck, tough shit, horse shit* and *bull shit* were not easy for me to comprehend. So many slang expressions did not make sense to me. *Shoot the breeze, shoot the bull, shut eye*, which really should be "eyes shut," or *let's hit the hay*, and similar phrases caused me many sleepless nights. Often, I had to ignore the confusion and go on; otherwise, my mind would have been so distracted that I could not have concentrated on my daily studies and duties.

Trying to make sense out of *awful nice, awful good, awful cold, awful kind, pretty cold, pretty hot, pretty ugly, pretty stupid, pretty sharp, pretty loose, pretty tight, pretty wild, pretty sad, pretty lousy* and many more confusing idioms caused me months of puzzlement. Those who grow up with these expressions don't think about any of this at all, but, for most foreigners trying to learn English, many of these slang expressions would be extremely hard to figure out. If something or someone is "pretty" how can it also be "pretty ugly?" What kind of weather is supposed to be "pretty cold or pretty hot?" Then we say, "awful smart" and "awful pretty."

Is it " pretty silly" or "awful silly?" How can "pretty bad" and "awful bad" be the same? Using, misusing and abusing some words have obviously changed the actual meaning of them. *Pretty* does not mean pretty any more, it often means *fair*: If someone asked you how you rated this book, please don't say *pretty good* which means it was fair or so so. Not excellent, and not bad. I would much rather hear, it was *awfully good!* How ironic that "awful" comes across as seeming better than "pretty." Wow, that *sounds pretty bad.* And of course, using the word *bad* for *good* and visa versa, causes additional confusion. For example, you scared me *pretty bad* means exactly the same as: you scared me *pretty good*! How could that be? It just did not make sense to me and such idiosyncrasies made me think that getting an advanced degree in America might be out of my reach.

You might be interested to learn that the dictionary offers six definitions for " awful:"
1: inspiring-awe, 2: highly impressive, 3: causing fear-terrifying, 4: dreadful-appalling 5: full of awe-reverential, 6: very bad-ugly- unpleasant. Honestly, I did not know which meaning I was supposed to pick.

After a while I tried to be creative in order to make sense out of some of these slang expressions. For instance I thought *pretty ugly* would be used in referring to a person who has a pretty face but an ugly personality. In the same way I thought that *pretty fat* is probably used for people with a beautiful face and a large body, and the opposite is, of course, *pretty skinny*!

Just as I was getting *pretty proud of myself* and wanting *to toot my horn* for figuring things out, I heard another bit of slang that made me *stop dead.* That was *pretty shitty.* Wow! How was I supposed to translate that one?

For the first two years, I often at midnight would go out into the freezing streets of Laramie to cry by myself. In that solitude and loneliness I was able to force myself to stay focused on other things rather than on what was an otherwise miserable state of mind. My only comfort came from knowing that my family slept peacefully without knowing what I went through day and night. Needless to say, the windy, cold, icy streets of Laramie were not the most comfortable places to seek a solution, but where else did I have to go?

To get my driver's license in Laramie the first time was a *kick.* I did fine on the written test even though it took me a long time to complete. However, the conversation for the rest of the process was strange. When the official asked me, how tall I was, I answered 170, as I only knew my measurements in metric. This, *threw* the officer *off balance* and he had to ask me again. When I repeated the same centimeters, he shook his head and said "We'll say five-ten." Confused, he continued, "Tell me how much you weigh, without being funny!" My answer was 77, of course in kilograms. He was losing his patience with me and said, "Do you think that you are a comedian? Hurry up, I have other people waiting in line, will you?" I did not know what to say, so I kept quiet innocently looking at him. He *gave up on me* and said, "Oh, well, *what the heck*, I don't have a whole day *to mess with you*, we'll just put 175."

He took my picture and said, "Now comes the worse part." I asked why? He replied. "because I have to *hit you with four bucks*." I thought to myself, here we go again with the boxes! The man saw that I didn't understand him. He took a dollar out of his pocket and said "I want four of these." People in the room started giggling, but in an embarrassing way I finally learned what *bucks* meant!

During my third week at the University of Wyoming, the assistant director of the athletic department handed me a key for a university car and the schedule for coaches meeting at Regis College in Denver. I had no idea how difficult finding our meeting place in a big city would be! Proudly, I took my wife and daughter along hoping the trip would be a nice outing for us. It ended up a nightmare. I drove from one end of Denver to the other several times without finding the College. People were nice in giving me directions; it was I who had a hard time following them. "*Hang a right, hang a left, overpass, underpass.*" When it came to parking, I could not figure out why people were allowed to "*drive in the parkway* but had to *park in the driveway.*" I thought it had to be the other way around!

My understanding of the word "hang" was "to attach something above with no support from below." Therefore *hang a right* or *hang a left* were practically Greek to me. Imagine my surprise and confusion when I heard similar slang expressions: *get the hang of it, hang around, hang about, hang back, hang fire, hang five, hang ten, hang in there, hang loose, hang tight, hang on, hang one on, hangout* as one word, then *hang out* as two words, *hang over*, two words, but *hangover* as one word, *hang to, hang together, hang tough, hang up, not give a hang about*. My goodness it's enough to make one's *head spin* with so many meanings and various uses of *hang* in English, but one thing I know for certain, if you *let it all hang out*, you will be arrested. At last, *I get* why after so many years of studying English, I still cannot *get the hang of it*!

Speaking of "*get*" or "*got*" could be a chapter by itself. There are 22 meanings of *get* in the dictionary, and to *add a little icing to the cake*, or to the confusion Americans say: *get about, get around, get across, get after, get along, get around to, get at, get away, get away with, get back, get behind, get by, get down, get down to, get in, get on, get on it, get it, get it on, get nowhere, get off, get off on, get one off, get out, get out of, get over, get somewhere, get over it, get there, get here, get through, get to, get together, get up* and more.

Do you *get my drift*? And if I haven't put you *over the edge* by now, here are a few more to think about. *Gotta go*; Shirley *is not getting it, got it*? He *got off the subject; John is a go getter; it gets me*, and how was I supposed to understand the meaning of: *when the going gets tough, the tough get going?*

My neighbor, Wayne asked me, "Parviz, *you get any last night*?" Often to be polite to people I just said "yes" or "no" without really understanding fully what was being asked. So, I replied, "yes." Suddenly, he *punched me in the arm* and said "*you devil you*," I stood there staring at him not knowing what that was all about!

On another occasion, he asked me, "Parviz, I want you to do me a big favor." Being the helpful young man that he was, I replied, "Sure, whatever you need; I would be happy to do it for you." He said, I am jealous of you, you seem to always have *your shit together*. I need your help in getting *my shit together*!" I thought that such a statement was not a nice thing to say to a friend, as I considered it an ugly request. Then, I looked at him in a disgusted way and said "Moslems *do not touch their shit*."

136

I have always had a fascination with other cultures and languages. Although I only spoke four languages and understood two more, I was considered a *"goof ball"* in my family. My father spoke seven languages fluently and most of my siblings knew five or more. Educated people in Iran learn a second or third language for several reasons, but mainly for vacationing and travel in foreign countries.

However, in spite of my linguistic skills, to earn a degree in a second language or to pursue a career and to compete in the work place with native speakers is a monumental challenge.

Every language has its complications, especially in areas of pronunciation and in sentence structures, but most of all in slang or idiomatic expressions. According to Webster's New World Dictionary, English is the most difficult language to master.

My American wife has tried to learn a few words in Farsi to impress my mother. One of the phrases she wanted to learn was, "How are you?" After practicing several times with me, she said, *shotory*. *Chetory* or *shotory*, does not sound too different does it? However, one is a polite question the other is an insult meaning "you are a camel."

I smile when I remember hearing for the first time "Sue *heard it straight from the horse's mouth.*" I realize that many of these expressions make perfect sense to those of you who grew up with them; however, it did not sound right to me. And in fact, years later, I obviously got one of these expressions wrong, because not feeling well, I said to my American wife, "I have a *horse* in my throat." She looked at me, as only wives can, and said, "No, you have a *hoarse* throat." But the man standing next to us said to my wife, "No, you are wrong, he means he has a *frog* in his throat."

British English is normally taught to students living outside of the United States. Generally, emphasis has been placed on grammar, conjugation, punctuation, or pronunciation. Learning slang, and conversational skills which I found to be probably the most important for survival in America are often not emphasized or are overlooked. I had passed all the required tests for English competency before I came to the Unites States. But when I landed in New York City, the English language I knew, did not help me much in my communication. I suddenly felt dumb and seriously wondered if I knew enough English to earn my graduate degree.

While "look" and "see" are similar in meaning, *overlook* is opposite to *oversee*. The latter is to look at carefully, and the former means to not "see." Likewise, to be called a *wise man* is a compliment and a *wise guy* is an insult.

The first time I heard two of my classmates gossiping about a female acquaintance, saying *she's been around the block a couple of times,* I didn't know why they were making fun of her. But the way they said it made me feel rather uncomfortable .

I told them they should be proud of her for trying to stay in shape. They didn't understand me and in a sarcastic manner replied: "We mean she is *loose* Parviz, *loose as a goose*." That, *threw me off.* I said, "What's wrong with that? They should try to do some exercise and stretching, it would do wonders for them." They stared at me as if I were *dumber than a box of rocks.*

The plural of *man* is *men*, however, *pan* is *pans; goose* is *geese,* but *moose* isn't *meese*, it's simply *moose.* And *deer* is *deer,* whether it is one or one hundred! And you wonder why I, and many other foreigners, *go bananas,* trying to learn English.

I cannot describe my sense of bewilderment when a classmate told me jokingly; *"Put it where the sun doesn't shine!"* I honestly thought he wanted to put something of his in the shade to avoid sun damage. Furthermore, when I asked him what he wanted me to put where, his response was, *"you can put it up your zoo zoo. Ah, ain't* youth and the *good ol'* college days *grand*!

Seeing the look on my face, a friend feeling sorry for me, told the first person; "When you talk to this *poor guy*, you better *mind your manners* and *watch your P's and Q's*. I did not appreciate his referring to me as a *poor* guy. And, you guessed it! I didn't know what *minding your manners* or *watch your P's and Q's* meant. I knew that a "mind" is found in a person's brain, but had no idea how it fit with "manners," which mean customs and etiquette of social life. *Peas*, I knew, because soup can be made with them. In short, I couldn't make *heads or tails* out of Q's.

Based on <u>Webster's New World Dictionary</u>, "Variation within a language is of two main kinds. From one kind, we identify those who use the language. We infer where they come from, what groups they belong to, when they learned the language, and what they are like as individuals, their age, sex, education, and personality. Such variation is called dialect. From the other kind, we identify the uses into which language is put: the subject it treats, the circumstances in which it is used, the medium of its expression (for example, speech versus writing), the social relationships among its users, and the purposes of its use; such variation is called register.

The paradox of diversity in unity is more apparent in English than in any other language spoken upon the face of the Earth. The more widely a language is used, the more potential is has for variation. English, in the number of persons who use it, the geographical spread of its use, and the variety of purposes for which it is used, is the most popular language in the world.

Three groups of people use English: (1) those who speak it as a mother tongue, the first language they learn and the main one they use; (2) those who live in a bilingual environment or for whom English is a second language in frequent use in addition to their mother tongue; and (3) those for whom English is a foreign language used for special purposes."

As an aside, I sincerely believe it is a necessity for those who come to America or for that matter if they go to any other country to learn the *darn* language. This is the least they can do in payment for the advantages and opportunities they have gained. If they try to learn the language they would not be an additional burden to their new country nor an embarrassment to themselves.

Writing a book in a second language is a *"horse of a different color."* It took me 15 years to write my first book. Few would probably suffer the aggravation and frustration with the struggle of writing a text in one's second language. However, when I saw the book in print, my heartache and pain *flew out the window*, so to speak.

My continuous struggle with conquering English was not the only obstacle I had to overcome in America. There were numerous other problems that made me equally miserable at times. But, I can proudly say, quitting has never been in my vocabulary. I was determined to be successful regardless of how tough the *going got.*

Unfortunately for me, I had a narrow-minded advisor at UW, the dean, who placed me in an unpleasant position. He not only disliked foreigners, he felt the same way about the athletic department. Needless to say, I had *two strikes* against me. My successful coaching and winning team gave him additional ammunition to dislike me. Talking with him or asking for an appointment became next to impossible and created a very *tough situation* for me.

In addition, having a wife who hated America and Americans made for its own dreadful living conditions at home. She cried constantly for the first three years, wanting to go back to Iran and her mother. That alone was enough to *drive me crazy*.

It would have been nice just once to hear a "thank you" for the sacrifices I made in getting my family out of Iran and continued to make in the United States to give her and our daughter a life where freedom, human rights and equality are the norm. One does not need to be a *rocket scientist* to understand the difference between the life of a woman in Iran then (and sadly now under the harsh, restrictive Islamic government) and the freedoms a woman can enjoy in America.

My family and I could have lived in student housing, which

was more affordable, but Hava insisted on having a house. Trying to please her, I was forced to work as a busboy in a cafeteria, a lift operator at a Wyoming ski resort, and at a gas station to *make ends meet*. We were living *life on a shoe string*. Even though our family in Iran was wealthy, capable of helping us, no one ever offered. I would have been more than glad to have paid them back with interest, but none of them expressed a desire to lend a hand. And so, I accepted jobs and did work that I had never done in my life before.

Ironically enough, because of the political unrest in Iran, these same relatives kept sending their teenagers to America and, of course, to live with us. Some shipped their sons and daughters out of Iran to avoid military service. At different times I was the home-away-from-home parent for seven children ranging from six to eighteen years old. Attending PTA meetings alone became a full-time position. We never had a dull moment with these teenagers, who were wild, rebellious, and often in trouble at school.

Pressure from the SAVAK to ensure my timely return after graduation made for additional stress in my new country. Professional torture experts knew how to frighten and intimidate Iranians. The SAVAK operating in America had the power to kill, kidnap, and torture many Iranians. Several times, I had *"cold feet"* not knowing what to do when they whisked my daughters away in an effort to warn and scare me. The first incident occurred with Sima while we were visiting Universal Studios in Los Angeles. They stood there holding her hand while saying to me, "If you don't go back soon, you may lose your daughter."

The second incident was in Boulder, Colorado with my younger daughter, Eli. She was about 4 or 5 years old and standing next to me in a grocery store while I reached for a can of soup, reading the ingredients to be sure there was no pork in it, as well as the cooking directions. When I turned back to Eli, she was not there. Frightened, I started to look for her to see where she was but found no sign of her. This was not like Eli,

141

as she had always been a thoughtful child who would not wander away without telling me. The aisles were empty and I thought that I should have seen her by now if she were in the store.

In my worried state of mind, a very well dressed gentleman in a business suit and dark sun glasses tapped me on the shoulder and said to me in Farsi, "Eli is in the car with my partner," apparently another SAVAK agent. He asked me for a definite date for my return to Iran. Then he added that they had no plans for harming my daughter, but that if I did not give them a specific date soon, the next time I would see Eli would be in Tehran. I was astounded! This agent had suddenly appeared out of nowhere. I was speechless. I felt a new *all time low* realizing that it would take a miracle to be free of the "claws" of the Shah and Iran. They had made their point and let Eli out of their Mercedes, her hands full of chocolate candies. I held her in my arms, softly crying as they drove away.

This ordeal caused me many sleepless nights and when I finally did sleep, I had horrible nightmares. It is unimaginable for most Americans to visualize how dreadful life under a dictatorship can be. Today in 2003 and after the war with Iraq, some Americans are beginning to understand how terrible life is without human rights, and more specifically, how brutal Saddam's treatment of his own people was.

Fortunately, I knew how to deal with their system, so I planned to pacify the SAVAK. I was able to buy time by satisfying his Majesty, the Shah, with my accomplishments in America. I did this by giving lectures about the great "king of kings" to prove my loyalty to the government. Subsequently, I received the honorary title of most outstanding student abroad in 1971 from the Iranian Embassy. In addition, my success in training American athletes, who became recognized champions, satisfied his Majesty and he ordered the SAVAK to leave me alone, at least for a while. Fortunately, the Islamic revolution took the Shah's power and control away, and he was no longer able to pressure his citizens or me. Finally, after twelve years of living in fear, I felt free in America!

Regretfully, I lost my chance of earning my doctoral degree from the University of Northern Colorado because I took too long. Most American universities allow only seven or eight years for completion of a Ph.D. Later, I started all over again at the University of Denver.

Earning my master's degree at the University of Wyoming was not easy. Dealing with my adviser, the dean of the school of physical education, was more complicated than I had anticipated. At the beginning Dr. Smith showed an admirable, helpful attitude toward my family and me. Frequently he stated that he understood my position in trying to work and earn a degree in a second language. He also made me promise before purchasing anything to ask him first. He insisted that he had many extra things in his garage which he would be more than happy to lend to me. He specifically spoke about a crib which I could use for Sima, and many academic books which I needed for my classes. He shared with me his religious beliefs that the crib, however, could not be given away as it would mean they would have more children, but I could borrow it.

Two months later when he saw me driving my new 1967 Dodge Dart, he gave me a look as if I had done something wrong, perhaps deceived him. Afterward, getting appointments with him for consultations was next to impossible. He simply avoided me. In my sincere efforts to try to figure out what had gone wrong, other faculty members stated that they had overheard Dr. Smith discussing my dishonest dealings with him. He thought that there was no need to borrow a crib and his books if I was capable of buying a brand new car. Quite simply, I didn't fit his stereotype of a student from the Middle East, living on welfare and handouts from Americans. As he could no longer talk to me rationally, I was forced to request a change in advisors.

Even though I returned Dr. Smith's crib and books promptly, the distance between us remained. He could not let go of his resentment and he made life difficult for me in any

143

way that he could.

Once he accused his secretary of giving me a copy of his test. His unjust accusation made her break down in tears, and other faculty members had to come to her defense. He believed that with all the intelligent students in his class there was no way that a foreigner, who could barely speak English, could score the highest. One of the faculty members who was trying to calm the dean down told him, "Dr. Smith, the foreigner who you are referring to, was the only student to hand in a perfect paper in my statistics class."

The other professor, Dr. Jones, who was waiting to have his say, told Dr. Smith, "You must set aside some time to discuss academic subjects with Parviz. If you would, you will learn that he is very knowledgeable and interesting person. I am sure you would respect him, regardless of his place of birth, instead of looking down on him." Dr. Jones continued in his mild manner to prove his point further. "In sixteen years of teaching my class on Organizing and Managing University Intramurals, Parviz gave me a helpful idea and made me realize for the first time that it is never too late to learn. He illustrated in the class that by reversing the bracket in the second half of the competition, none of the teams would have to play each other twice."

Worrying about the preparation required for taking the GRE (Graduate Record Exam) was so stressful that often I had difficulty breathing and my heart would race. I scored the lowest in the verbal section (knowledge of English), while earning one of the highest grades in aptitude (mathematics and geometry) in the school of education. The test was so strenuous that it leaves a person drained, exhausted, numbed and mumbling to himself afterward.

In my opinion, a multiple choice test reflects more of an individual's comprehension of English rather than control of the subject matter. I was so upset by one of my tests that I became physically ill. This happened with a simple, multiple choice test. One choice was: "a *sound mind* in a *sound body*." The

144

only meaning for *sound* I knew at the time was noise. I did not understand how a mind could be "noisy." Yet, I still had to figure out what they meant by "noisy body." My lips turned blue, my face was pale, and my eyes were dilated. My heart was beating so loud that anyone close to me could hear it. Worrying about this caused me to feel faint.

In my desperate state of mind I tried to think of some connection between "sound," "mind" and "body." Using my logic and creativity, I interpreted it in this way: if a person's joints crack or if passes loud gas, this could be referred to as body noise. But I could not find an explanation for a mind making or being a sound!

Fortunately, professor Gill noticed my ashen face. Being a considerate gentleman and a great teacher he wanted to know why I looked ill. I was in the middle of the first page of a five page test when he approached me. Some students had already finished the test and were handing in papers. Watching them leave caused me further anguish, aware of my own lack of speed in reading and writing English. I became so nervous that I could not focus on answering the questions.

The professor asked me if I felt all right. I first thanked him, then said, "I'm, okay, sir, but would you please be kind enough to tell me how a mind can be noisy?" He felt terrible and with compassion, he apologized and asked me to hand him my papers. He said that I should take his test orally the next day. I did, and I received an A because of his clear explanation of each question. My written test could not have been better than a D, or more likely an F.

Some amenable professors granted me a few extra minutes here and there, while others did not allow me one minute longer than the set time, as they justified that it would not be fair to the others. I respected their decision, but wondered how they would have scored if the positions were reversed.

The following are a few adages in English that illustrate the difficulty that I, and other immigrants, have. Explanations are not needed as to the difference in meaning, but notice should be

145

taken also of the difference in pronunciation.

The soldier decided to *Desert* his *Dessert* in the *Desert.*

The Insurance was *Invalid* for the *Invalid.*

After a *Number* of injections my jaw got *Number.*

When shot at, the *Dove Dove* into the bushes.

The *Wind* was too strong to *Wind* the sail.

A seamstress and a *Sewer* fell down into a *Sewer* line.

The buck *Does* funny things when the *Does* are around.

Upon seeing the *Tear* in the painting I shed a *Tear.*

The farm was used to *Produce Produce.*

How can I *Intimate* this to my most *Intimate* friend.

I spent last *Evening Evening* out a pile of dirt.

If a person says *the stars are out,* he means every star is visible, but when he says the *lights are out*, he means nothing is visible.

The "satem" language of Iranian is quite different from the "centum" languages, such as English. In the former, writing is from right to left with a different alphabet that has no similarity to the Latin alphabet. Dots placed above or below a letter can change the meaning of a word from negative to positive and vice versa. For instance, in Farsi this word بکن means "do it" and this word نکن means "don't." The word بکش means "kill him;" by placing the dot at the top نکش, it changes the meaning to "do not kill him."

Language is the main reason that a great majority of foreign students in America choose majors in engineering or architectural fields which would not require such a high proficiency in English. Calculating mathematical numbers for a building or handling a design drawing for a construction project is easier than preparing for a course in advanced psychology, philosophy, or literature. Subjects that require a solid background in English are too difficult for students from other countries to succeed in.

I had no problem earning high grades in mathematic-based classes. Statistics and research courses were a *piece of cake.* I had to change my minor from school administration to statistical research because I found it much easier to earn an A in those courses than school law or similar subjects. I earned enough A's in mathematics to bring my grade point average up for graduation.

Once for a test, I needed to borrow an eraser from a student next to me. I asked him if I could use it. He answered, "*You betcha.*" I did not know what he meant. I waited a bit and asked him again. This time he said, "You *bet*," but I still did not make the association. The word "bet," as it is used for betting or wagering, in reference to use of his eraser didn't make sense to me. I asked him, "Does "bet" mean yes or no?" He suddenly realized that I didn't understand his reply and he apologized while laughing.

The disturbance brought our professor over to my desk. The conversation was related to him and he laughed too. When I saw both of them laughing, I felt humiliated not knowing if they were making fun of me. It was yet another uncomfortable situation for me.

Occasions like this created an unending negative perception of myself in my mind. From being a famous athlete in Iran, nationally admired, where fans loved to talk to me, shake my hand, and ask for my autograph, to having folks constantly laugh at me in my new country, was a *tough* transition. It made me feel like a clown. Being made fun of on that particular day, while I was struggling to focus on my test, consequently affected my concentration, and caused me not to score as high as I could have.

I became friends with a classmate, Pam, who needed my help with her statistics class. In return, she did a wonderful job in preparing me for subjects, such as Psychology, Philosophy, and other classes which required more English comprehension and in which I needed a tutor. Once when Pam was explaining something to our professor, she told him, "Parviz is *pulling my leg.*" That made me angry. It was important for me to let her and Dr. Hill know that I had not touched her leg, as I was a

147

married man. She laughed in response saying, "*Oh, yeah*, you *always like to pull my leg*." Her last words, along with both of them laughing, embarrassed me. I said angrily, "Listen, lady, you should be careful about who is playing with your leg, instead of accusing me." I also wanted to ask about the meaning of her saying, "oh, yeah."

Frequently, I felt that people were making me seem like a fool which made me very self conscious. I was bothered, upset, and annoyed. I did not know if they were laughing at my clothes, at my accent, the many questions I always asked, or just because of my problems in conversations. In this particular case, I felt that Dr. Hill and Pam thought I was lying. I was hurt and could not understand why someone as nice as Pam would accuse me of touching her leg. I left the room. My friend ran after me, begging me to stop so she could explain that *pulling my leg* is an innocent expression; it did not mean a physical touch.

Along with her apology, Pam mentioned that she could not *stand hurting my feelings*. Her explanation did not make sense at all, as I did not see a relation between *standing* or *sitting* and what it had to do with "feelings." *Pulling my leg* became a *standing joke* in our class for the rest of that semester. The only joke I heard about "sitting" in that class was: you can *sit on it*!

With my coaching assistantship at the University of Wyoming, I had to teach a few Physical Education classes as well. Since all my correspondence with the University had been by mail, I was not aware of the details or perhaps had been too excited to ask. All I knew was that I would be teaching some activity classes, which seemed fine. But the published teaching schedule at the campus indicated more involvement than I had presumed. One was teaching soccer, which was my strongest area of expertise. However, when I saw "touch football," I felt faint hearted. How could they do this to me? I had never even seen a ball the shape of an American football. I wanted to find the party responsible for putting me in such an awkward position. I knew absolutely nothing about football!

Other faculty members, trying to help, explained that it was common practice to offer two different activities in an 18-week standard semester. Nine weeks of soccer, and nine weeks of touch football. I could not convince anyone how ridiculous it was to expect me to teach a sport that I had never played before, nor had a clue about the rules or strategies of the game. As a matter of fact, I had never even watched a football game on television!

Their unanimous answer was, "We all have taught soccer, which we know nothing about. It is not a *big deal*, don't worry. A couple of them said: " All you have to do is group the boys in teams to play against each other. They know how to play and what to do. For grades, we give the winning team an 'A' the second place a 'B,' and 'C' for the rest, to make it simple."

In a way their advice gave me a little comfort to realize that educating the students in physical activities was not a big concern! I really did not know what else I could do. In another way their proposal upset me, thinking that if this was the standard of grading in the American educational system there must be something wrong. I could not convince them that my case was different. My fear stemmed from teaching football to Americans who grew up with the sport. *How odd* that their instructor was the one who didn't know the sport!

Fortunately, after the first nine weeks of teaching soccer I earned the respect of my students. Never having been taught soccer in a professional manner before, my students really enjoyed playing the game for the first time in their lives. The news of my varsity team's winning streak gave them confidence in my teaching ability. However, their respect and confidence was not enough to rescue me when I had to make *tough judgment calls* in football to resolve a conflict. I held my clipboard, walking around the field, pretending to know what I was doing. It gave me some *breathing room* to take notes for myself about the game of football. Everything seemed fine as long as there were no disputes or cheating. My nightmares began when the players were arguing about *a call* and came to me for the answer. Even now, after more than thirty six years, I remember some of those incidents and I laugh at how hysterical they were.

One day, the players came to me shouting and arguing so loudly that it was hard for me to understand what they were talking about. They were saying, "Coach, they *fumbled* the ball on the *line of scrimmage*; we recovered it, don't *we get the ball*?" The other team was insisting that, "No, they get the *down*." I did not have a clue what they were arguing about. If I didn't know what they were asking, how could I settle it for them? I had to ask for a little more explanation, starting with, "Who fumbled the ball?" "Peter did, coach, *right on the line of scrimmage* and we recovered it." I had several problems: one, what was fumble?, two, how could they recover it?, and, three, where was this so called line of scrimmage?

To play it *cool* I faced Peter, holding my hands on my hips, asking him, "Why did you fumble the ball; don't you know that you are not supposed to?" I thought that fumble must be some sort of foul play or illegal procedure, not unintentionally dropping the ball. My blaming Peter surely confused the students. They thought either I was a comedian or a *nut*. Of course at that time I did not know that a "nut" could also mean foolish or better yet, a *fruit cake*! But, none of this mattered, because the conflict was not being resolved. Then, I ordered them to replay. Not understanding how to replay a "fumble" caused the boys even more puzzlement. Was Peter supposed to let the ball drop out of his hands again, to see if the other team could recover it? From what point in the game were they supposed to "replay" it!

Regardless of what I said or how I tried to settle the argument, I could not *put an end* to their problem. Truly, I *confused the hell* out of them. But how can a person confuse the "hell" out of them if it is supposed to be a place, not a mind or a person?

Since I was hearing the boys arguing about two different

things, *down* and *ball*, I came up with a brilliant idea to *settle that mess* in a fair manner. I ordered them with full authority that one team must have the "down" and the other should get the "ball," and let's *get on with the game*! Everyone laughed, telling me I was "a *funny guy*." Luckily, I was *saved by the bell*, as they left for their next class chuckling about the episode.

That was the time I learned the expression *"Hit the road, Jack,"* when one student said it to a teammate who did not want to stop playing. Seeing an end to a *helluva mess* made me run as fast as I could to the locker room to find a faculty member and ask for help. This incident saved me for the rest of the semester, as the students never wanted to waste playing time coming to the "coach" for the answer to a predicament.

On my way to the locker room I stopped by the office to pick up my messages. I saw a nice, young boy of about ten years old standing next to our secretary. She wanted me to meet him, and proudly asked me "if I had met her *offspring*?" I slowly and hesitantly responded, "No." She smiled and said, "Parviz, meet my youngest son."

Financially the *going got tough*, and I needed to earn extra money. The living expenses of a family and going to school were difficult to manage. Hava, as a Persian wife, did not believe that it was correct to work outside of the home; thus, we needed more income. Being a *busboy* in a dorm cafeteria was not enough. I had to seek additional work. The recreation department in school coincidentally needed softball umpires for their summer program. They could not find enough students willing to apply; so, they thought I should apply to help the department and myself.

The pay was encouraging, but I could not even think of accepting the position because I had no idea what softball was *all about*. I had never played it, never watched it, did not know what the playing field looked like, how the game was played or how to keep score. Cliff, the recreational director, tried his best to convince me to accept the job. Of course, his thinking was typically American, and he assumed that I would know softball. His assumption was true for those who lived in countries where baseball is played. With or without playing the game themselves, most would know how baseball is played. I did not have the slightest idea about it. He could not understand why I would turn down his generous offer, knowing I was desperately looking for part-time work everywhere. Having no other applicants for the position made Cliff more desperate than I. Gladly, I would have taken the job, if there were a way, because I needed the money as badly as he wanted an umpire.

He skillfully convinced me to take one of the positions based on his teaching me everything about softball. Cliff promised me I would like it. Furthermore, I could quit any time if I did not. Stupidly I agreed and he was thrilled. He shook my hand in agreement and said, *"Trust me*, you won't have any problem since softball is the simplest game in the world." We made an appointment for the following day. He spent approximately 20 minutes teaching me about softball. I learned how the game was played, the rules and whatever he thought I needed to know. He drew the field on the blackboard, showing me the bases to demonstrate how players hit the ball and run around those bases to score.

Admittedly, Cliff's thorough explanations *impressed the heck out of me*. He also handed me a piece of paper that contained in writing what he had said about the game so I could have it as my rule book. His instructions were easy to understand. It was the first time I heard about scoring, *balls, strikes, home runs, in or out, innings*, etc.

Before my first game I went to watch other games being played. I decided that by observation I could make myself a better umpire. Everything seemed to be going well, and I started to feel confident. Suddenly I heard one umpire call, *"Foul ball!"* Cliff never mentioned "foul ball" to me. I became nervous, *broke out in a sweat*, and began to wonder how many other terms he might have forgotten to teach me. I ran to him and said, "You must forgive me, I'm going home, there is no way that I can referee."

The poor man could not understand what *was the matter with me*. He told me I was not being fair, since I had promised him to give it a try. He did not have a substitute to umpire my game. Then he added, "Would you please explain why you want to quit? Did I do something wrong, are you ill, can I do anything to change your mind?" I was terrified and said, "You never told me anything about "foul balls" and I am not sure how many other things you forgot to tell me." Cliff laughed but said, "I'm sorry, I forgot that simple term; it is not a problem to worry about. Foul ball is like a strike, it's only a ball hit out of the playing field from the side lines when we call it foul ball. Also, if the ball touches the bat but goes behind the hitter, instead of forward, into the playing field it is called foul ball. It is exactly the same as strike!" Parviz, you are a great referee in more complicated sports, such as basketball, volleyball, gymnastics, and soccer. *Trust me*, softball is nothing to be afraid of. You will do just fine.

Cliff was absolutely right, but he left out *a thing or two*. He convinced me to *stick with it*. My first few games were simple and I learned a lot from the players. It was a new experience for me to learn about the American temper, mood, tough times with losing and cussing. I hardly had to call anybody "out" after three strikes. The players would just throw their bats and say some words which began with "f", "g," or "sh," and walk away.

My worst nightmare happened in the sixth game. I was going to call a player "out" because of three strikes (two strikes and a foul ball, which I was told was the same as a strike). I was quite surprised noticing that he did not throw his bat, he didn't cuss, and everyone seemed to be happy to continue. The pitcher was on the mound, the catcher crouched behind the plate, and the batter was ready to hit. This confused me, thinking that I might have made a mistake in counting. Looking at my notes on the clipboard, I recounted his strikes. I was right, he had three strikes. I told myself, maybe the players had counted incorrectly. I decided if everyone was happy with it I should not say a thing and let him have another strike, so what? That *son of a gun* had one more foul ball, making it four strikes according to my count.

Again, no one reacted in the usual angry way, throwing the bat, using bad words. I forced myself to *keep my trap shut* again, since everyone seemed happy without any complaints. I just *let it slide*. His fifth foul ball (strike) made me *lose it*. I called him "out" and told him he had five strikes. That created such a hilarious scene on the playing field that the game had to be stopped until everyone could quit laughing. The batter, who was a very nice, young man, assured me that if I would just keep quiet, he would step aside when he had three strikes.

In my lifelong pursuit of learning English, I experienced innumerable misinterpretations that caused awkward and negative situations for myself and others.

But on the other hand, I met and was befriended by many kind and wonderful people in not only Laramie, but also in the many other places I called "home" in the United States. My family and I found very caring and generous people in Greeley, Longmont, Vail, and Twin Lakes, Colorado. These gracious people invited us into their homes, frequently took my daughters to ball games or parks, and did their best to make Hava feel welcomed. Because of their genuine warmth and hospitality, leaving my family and friends in Iran was not as *wrenching* as it could have been. At the time, I did not have the opportunity or know the right words to express my deep appreciation to each and every one of the fantastic people who invited us to their parties, Thanksgiving dinners, Christmas festivities, and other special family occasions. Now, through this book, I would like them to know that they were my main support system in my new country, and I am forever grateful.

One of the fun parties we were invited to I remember as if it were only yesterday. As we walked into the house, we saw the women were in the kitchen preparing the food, having a cocktail, and *munching on goodies*. The men were *glued to the TV* in the family room, drinking beer, cheering and cussing with

154

every play. They shouted from the room, "Hey, coach, we're here watching the ball game, come on back!" I did not know what game they were watching, so I asked, "What game and who is playing?" *The Twins* someone shouted. Naturally, I needed a bit more information so I asked, "Which twins?" "Minnesota Twins" was the answer. I said, "Their mother must be very proud of them." They *didn't get it* and started laughing, thinking that I was making a joke. A few looked at me in a weird way, as if I were from another planet. The host introduced me to the rest as a *funny guy* with a good sense of humor!

Their thinking of me as being funny, when I hardly knew enough English *to get by*, recently gave me the idea to write a book about my experiences, to give lectures with a humorous slant, and to bring laughter to people. Now that I am retired I have time to reflect on my life and being an educator at heart I will always want to share and inspire if I can.

As a coach, I had a hard time avoiding questions such as, what did I think about the *World Series*? Who did I think was going to *get it*? Get what? My innocent and naive answers gave them a peculiar impression of what kind of a teacher I was. So, when I answered "they would be better off looking the "World Series" up in an encyclopedia for the best answer, they were baffled and did not know what to think of me.

My ignorant replies, along with their good nature, were the reasons for people introducing me as a very funny guy, thinking that I was purposely *throwing them a curve ball*. My reputation for having a great sense of humor, combined with lack of interest in watching the games like the other men, made me very popular with the women at the parties. I probably was the only male not glued to the television! *To add icing to the cake*, as an athlete I had a flat stomach, muscular legs and arms, a broad chest, with piercing blue eyes, curly black hair, and enough charm and good manners to win most American housewives' hearts.

In our gatherings the ladies made complimentary remarks

while *spoiling me to death*, with their homemade goodies. Their innocent flirting and teasing made Hava irate. She had a suspicious mind anyway, but her accusations were beyond imagination! She wrongfully thought I was having affairs with all of them; therefore, instead of enjoying herself, she had a miserable time. The intent of these parties was to let her know that she had friends and to make her feel welcome, but because of her insecurities and negative attitude she only became more depressed.

She seemed to not like me nor anyone or anything in America, which made my life quite stressful. If only Hava had exhibited a slight sign of appreciation to me for bringing her and Sima to America, I would have been happy. Her unjustified dislike of Americans became intolerable. No matter how hard I tried, I could not change her attitude. Whatever her personal reasons were, it created a growing distance between us that made the dissolution of our marriage inevitable. She complained and cried almost every day which made my coming home at night *a true hell*.

Speaking of *hell*, I often wondered how a simple four letter word could create such a *hell of a confusing* story. I had a *hell of a time* figuring out *what the hell* is the real meaning of this slang and *where and when the hell* it could be used properly. As a matter of fact, I could not find any place or occasion that people did not use it! To make sense out of many basic, routine conversations for me *was hell* up to this time. I never thought it was an item that you could give to anyone for punishment or reward.

The first association of "hell" in my mind and vocabulary was the ultimate rotten place, opposite to heaven, where wrong doers such as evil politicians, tyrants, terrorists, and killers are sent to burn in eternity. But *that was not it* in this country. This word seems to be used for everything good or bad, right or wrong, hot or cold.

Just for the hell of it, I would like to give you some examples: *To catch hell - to get hell -* my wife *gave me hell -*

Hell of a lady or *hell of a guy* - *hell of a day* - *hell of a deal* - the pianist gave *a hell of a concert*. *Fast as hell* - *slow as hell* - *sharp as hell* - *dumb as hell*. I had no problem with *hot as hell*, but believe me *cold as hell drove me crazy* to comprehend. *Hell you do* - *hell you don't* - *hell, yes* - *hell, no.*

If you think that wasn't confusing enough, *heck* is used interchangeably with *hell*. I am told that it is the more polite form of *hell*. Okay, if I am supposed to *buy that one* then please tell me, where is *heck?Heck you do* - *heck you don't* -*the heck* - *the hell or what the heck* -*what the hell*.

My neighbor Wayne could not stop bragging about the *hell of a deal he got on a car*. It puzzled me so much that I didn't know if I should congratulate him or feel sorry for his "hell of a deal." I also was not certain if *a hell of lady* was a good person or a woman of ill-repute.

Many simple words used in daily conversations *drove me bananas* or *messed me up pretty bad* or *pretty good*? I should *rest my case* and *quit while I'm ahead*. However, "resting my case" at the time meant *squat* to me since I thought a "case" was a container not a statement of the facts, as in a law court.

Languages normally follow the law of physics. For every action there is an equal and opposite reaction: *get in - get out*, get on - get off. Just as in physics, somethings make you sick and other things make you feel better. However, I have noticed in English that there are many statements or slang expressions which have no opposites. For example, I have heard, " my wife *drives me insane*," but never "she drives me sane." Many of these sayings, you probably never really think about, but for foreigners they create months of confusion and puzzlement.

The first year on campus I also had *a heck of a time* with "daylight savings." After a change to daylight savings time, I arrived at my early morning class to find the building locked and no one around. It *scared me half to death*, thinking that there must have been some sort of disaster or nuclear threat and that I should not be outside. In Iran we never changed the clock back and forth. As a matter of fact, in some other countries, the opening and closing times of businesses would be changed to concur to the difference in daylight.

The pressure of *keeping up* in graduate school, coaching, and holding down three part-time jobs was enough to *put me over the edge*. But it was the stress of my home life that finally *broke the camel's back*. Hava, with her impetuous behavior, forced me to withdraw the small amount of savings I had set aside for emergencies to buy two plane tickets for her and Sima to Tehran. In addition, I borrowed several thousands of dollars from a loan shark. Not having any established credit in America, I could not obtain a more reasonable rate for my loan from a bank. Against my better judgment, we agreed that I should stay and live in a dorm until graduation.

Her brilliant idea to save our marriage sounded great but it did not come to pass, because her desire to stay in Iran lasted only ten days. She quickly realized that Iran was not the place for a liberated female! Despite her expectations that life would be better in Tehran, she had tasted "freedom." Also, she missed me as her private chauffeur, grocery deliverer, and handyman. Living in Tehran on her own was her wake up call!

She hastily decided to get her passport back from the government, return to America, and surprise me. However, Iranian rules and regulations were more complicated than she expected. She needed a written, notarized permission submitted by her husband to validate her passport. This requirement created much complicated paperwork, as I was in the United States and overseas mail from the USA to Iran in 1968 would have taken more than a month. She wanted written permission from me that very day, as she could not wait ten more hours, let alone months, to get out of Iran.

Our daily lengthy, long distance calls to work out her problem from almost the other end of the globe lasted several weeks. Her new reason for crying was beyond my expectation. One long *winded conversation* dealt with her frustration with the system. It made her angry that a clergyman at the passport office would *not give her a break* and that he insisted on having

158

that "stupid" permission from me. Totally ignorant of her own country's way of life, where the officials created their own special sets of rules to get *kickbacks*, she could not convince him that her passport was needed to join her husband in America. But to Hava, this requirement seemed absolutely ridiculous and made her indignant.

She tried to express the magnitude of her frustrations on the phone, but, knowing the system, I could not stop laughing long enough to be sympathetic. I knew what the official had in mind in asking for such a document. She became quite angry with me and accused me of not being anxious in wanting to expedite the process. Hava expressed her resentment with the official's argument, who teased her saying, "Do you know how many husbands would *give an arm and a leg* to keep their wives away, far away?" With his final sarcastic remark of, "If I could send my wife to the moon with a one-way ticket, I would be the happiest man in the world," Hava just wanted to murder him. She had to control her temper, knowing she might never see her passport again if she upset him. Hava did not understand an Iranian government male worker's humor or his method of asking for money.

Iran's officials seemed to have a monopoly on corruption. A xerox copy of a birth certificate was not valid unless it had a stamp of verification from a clerk. Copies were supposed to be free because this was a government service. However, the official in charge made a profitable business out of it based on how many copies one needed and how soon! Knowing that a person needed copies immediately, the typical answer was, "Come back in two weeks." Naturally the question asked would be, "Is it possible to have it sooner?" The official would reply, "How soon?" while pulling open a desk drawer full of money, rolling his eyes toward the largest bills!

I had my first experience with that corrupt system when I was a freshman at the university. My soccer team was traveling to Europe for a tournament, and I needed two copies of my birth certificate for my passport. As a national champion, well known and highly respected in the country, I expected him to recognize me and understand how important and urgent it was. Ignorant of the system, I expected it to be easier for me, thinking I would be given the copies without any problems. How little did I know! At first I didn't understand his odd behavior, but quickly I realized that he was giving me subtle hints. As I appeared to not be getting his message, he decided to educate me. He told me to sit down in a chair next to him and began to make a *huge production over* how difficult it would be to get the copies to me sooner. Those already familiar with his system knew how to *grease the way* and communicate by dropping a bill in his drawer when asked how many copies or how soon the copies were needed. Based on the size of bills dropped in the drawer, the official would give a time for them to come back. To my utter surprise, I noticed that some people received their copies within minutes!

Those who did not pay or did not pay enough were told to come back in two to three weeks. After he was sure that I understood his little system, he asked me again, "Can you tell me now, when do you need your copies?" I dropped all the money I had in my pockets which was three *tomans* (Iranian dollars) in his drawer. Shaking his head, he disgustedly said, "I'll give your copies to you in a minute. You probably do not have the *bus fare* to come back and pick them up." I was not quite sure if I had *pissed him off* or had made him feel guilty.

In my wife's case, however, I knew how the system works but I was in America and her not knowing what to do became a big problem. After several attempts, I finally found out that it was possible to send my permission for her and Sima to return via airline special delivery. Unfortunately, her return did not solve the problem of improving our home life. She wanted my promise that I would take her to Iran every summer for visits until I graduated, at which time we would move there permanently. Honestly, I had every good intention to please her, but trips to Tehran each summer were out of the question, especially after the hassles and years it took for me to leave in

1967. I had no desire to go back at all.

After her return, a couple of our friends tried to help us by teaching her English in hopes of making our life easier. It did not change a thing. Many suggested that she should seek employment to force herself to speak English while earning an income. She did not want to hear of it. I managed to *hang in there* for months of a *topsy-turvy*, chaotic life. One day when our neighbor, Gloria, told Hava of a vacancy in their store, she displayed a sudden interest, which surprised me. Hava's inquiry about where to apply was pleasant news. She had always been a traditional Persian woman who did not work outside of the home. In fact, many never worked at all, having maids and servants doing everything for them.

Hava was hired at the store and for a short while she liked working there. The employees treated her nicely and provided a pleasant working experience for her. Once Hava made a display of *punch balls* by blowing them up and placing them in a cage. After she completed the display, a lady entered the store and asked her where in the store she could find some *punch bowls*. Not hearing the difference, Hava proudly took the customer to the cage full of balls, picked one out for demonstration and began punching it toward her face. The poor woman became frightened, thinking that Hava was a *crazy nut*, and ran out of the store. Hava's disappointment over the customer's response, instead of being appreciative of her helpfulness, puzzled her. Hesitant to tell anyone in the store, she waited at home for me to help her figure out the customer's strange behavior. It turned out to be quite an entertaining evening for me as I tried to explain the miscommunication. I was hoping that Hava would understand a bit of my own frustration in trying to get my doctoral degree in a second language.

Our first experience with Christmas parties in America took place at Hava's store. I was curious to learn how Americans celebrated a religious event. Naturally, having never been in such a situation, I expected that there would be praying or singing in a special, customary way. Contrary to my expectations, I had an interesting time watching people *getting smashed* on free booze. Two hours into the party, half of the guests, mostly men, could hardly stand up. The women were just getting *loosened up*. Their silly behavior, which I had never experienced before, amused me a great deal.

At Moslem parties and celebrations, the faithful are quite reserved, expressing their "love," behind closed doors, not in public. In addition, women are not permitted to exhibit sexual desires in front of others in Moslem countries. It is only in private that they can touch, caress, or kiss a man to express their affection. Culturally, the women have found a way to flirt and attract a man's attention in a public place. It is known as the "Middle Eastern Belly Dance" and females dance together, swaying and gyrating to the music in a sexual manner.

We have to accept that young people in other countries, which are not so sexually liberated as America, do some crazy things for "love" and create their own mode of adaptation for survival. For example, the cover that Moslem women wear known as a *chador*, an *abaya*, or a *burka* seems quite repressive to most Westerners and of course, more so to the liberated women of the United States. But this "cover" makes one "invisible" and it is the safest way for those women who wish to have a little *hanky panky* to avoid *getting caught*. Because of being completely covered from head to toe, no one knows who is going to whose house seeking a little extra spice in life. It is not uncommon for men to wear them also just to sneak to their lover's special meeting place. By "freeing" these women of their traditional cover, we, in fact, would be *messing up* their way of doing certain things. Any woman caught in extramarital affairs or in a sexual relationship if not married to that person would be punished severely, if not killed.

That Christmas party was quite an *eye-opener* for me. My being young, handsome, and sober was a plus during the festivities. I did not know the significance of mistletoe but was struck by the fact that some women were pulling me to a special spot, under a green leaf with berries and kissing me

162

quite seriously. A few held a green thing over my head and did the same. Besides being curious, I must confess that I enjoyed it, and did not try to stop them from sticking their tongues down my throat!

Hava, the reserved, jealous woman, became very angry with me. She insisted that we leave the party immediately. She once again accused me of having an affair with everyone even though she knew that I had not initiated any of these "actions" and that I didn't know most of their names.

Reviewing the first few years of being in my new country, I can truthfully say that it was not *a piece of cake*. The stress created by not being able to go forward or backward was killing me. In the centuries old Persian culture, there are words of wisdom for just about everything, and such a dilemma is referred to as "a saw up your ass," meaning I was stuck in a very painful position where I could not pull the saw out or push it in. Either way, it would hurt. I knew that I had serious problems and could not see a way to complete graduate school. Problems with English, lack of financial resources, and my unhappy life at home were my constant overwhelming concerns. There was no way I could go back to Iran without my doctoral degree and say, "I am sorry, your Majesty, but my plans did not work because I was incapable of earning a degree in America. Would you please forgive me and grant me a decent job?" Certainly, the chances of having a desirable position in Iran without my doctorate did not look good.

Many nights I walked the windy, freezing streets of Laramie from midnight until two or three in the morning hoping to find a solution. I could not *come up* with one. I cried each night by myself, not knowing what the next day would be like. I kept remembering my grandmother's promise that "there will be bright daylight after each long, dark, and cold night," but I began to doubt it. I had nowhere to go, no one to talk to and nothing to be cheerful about. The most stressful fact for me was the fear of not receiving a diploma because of my obvious disadvantage in English. My biggest problem centered on not being able to connect words together. I knew the meaning of them individually but could not make sense out of many sentences people used, such as:

I stuck my nose out the door. Don't stick your nose in my business. Bill was *drunk as a skunk.* Sue is a *screwed up mess.*

While the words *fat, slim* and *no* have entirely different meanings: *fat chance, slim chance* and *no chance* all mean the same. Many times I was left feeling as if I were *out to lunch*! Even reading funny jokes, instead of cheering me up, made me sad, because I didn't understand many of them. The following humorous play on words will give an example of my dilemma.

My first job was working in an orange juice factory,
 but I got *canned,* because I couldn't *concentrate.*
Then I worked in the woods as a lumberjack,
 but I just couldn't *hack it,* so they gave me *the ax.*
After that I tried to be a tailor, but I just wasn't
suited for it. Mainly because it was a *so-so* job.
Next I tried working in a muffler factory
but that was *exhausting.*
I wanted to be a barber, but I just couldn't *cut it.*
Then I tried to be a chef, figured it would add a little *spice*
to my life, but I just didn't have the *thyme.*
Finally, I attempted to be a deli worker,
but any way I sliced it, I couldn't cut the *mustard.*
My best job was being a musician,
but eventually I found I wasn't *noteworthy.*
I studied a long time to become a doctor,
but I didn't have any *patients.*
My next job was in a shoe factory;
I tried but I just didn't *fit in.*
I then became a professional fisherman,
but discovered that I couldn't live on my *net* income.
I managed to get a good job working for a pool
maintenance company, but the work was just too *draining.*

A number of my American friends played a significant role in trying to encourage me. They were aware of my academic struggles in school but had no knowledge of my painful home life. Pam, my studying partner, however, had an accurate educated guess. Even though I never mentioned a word about my personal turmoil, by her own intuition, she figured it out. Her terrific personality, great sense of humor, and her invaluable tutoring were the only encouragement I could count on those days.

Pam and I developed an unusual love/respect friendship for each other that rarely exists in this materialistic world. Our mutual enjoyment was pure and without expectations, which provided me with the added strength to go on. It enabled me to ignore my pain which was close to exceeding my human capabilities. Regretfully, our wonderful relationship abruptly ended.

One evening when I went to her apartment for our usual studying, I noticed that her living room had been transformed. The books on her dining table were replaced with candles, beautiful flowers, and a pretty place setting for two. She wore a sexy black dress, instead of her casual jeans and sweatshirt. I felt a kind of *love in the air* that I had not felt in years. My knees started shaking as my *heart jumped out of my rib cage*. I had dreamt about her often, thinking that *sharing love* with her would be wonderful. In English, people refer to this beautiful exchange of affection as *making love*, which to me was very unromantic and similar to *building* or *making* a cabinet.

Until that night, I thought that because I am a dreamer, my wishful thoughts were just figments of my imagination. But then I realized that something wonderful was about to happen. Apparently, she had the same feelings toward me and could not hide them any longer. Acting aggressively and getting right to the point while handing me a glass of wine, she said, "Parviz, *I don't mind if you are married*, let's have a toast tonight." Without thinking I asked her what she meant. I must have embarrassed her with my question, because she shook her head and said, "*Never you mind.*" I didn't know what she meant by that either, assuming that she might be implying that I had "no brain or no manners!"

But she was a very understanding and compassionate woman, aware of my difficulties with English. Gently, she changed the subject and tried to make me feel more comfortable. It was I who could not *let loose* or *get with the program.* I felt incapable of responding properly to her subtle hints. Regardless of her several "creative" translations to make me understand what she meant, I became more confused. Our communication, or the lack of it, affected my romantic mood. I was beginning to feel like an idiot.

After a few unsuccessful attempts, Pam said to me, "Would you like to *hit the hay with me?*" That did not make sense either, and I kept staring at her rather lost. Then she asked me bluntly if I knew what she wanted of me that night? I wanted so much to be "in love" and "loved" that I couldn't *think straight.* In my wild fantasies, I thought of undressing her, touching her, showing her my deep hidden desire and passion. But, I had no intentions of *fooling around* just *for kicks* so, as much as I wanted to share my love with Pam, I had to say no, and left her apartment. I had no desire to turn her life *upside down* nor make mine more complicated and painful than it already was.

My unexpected departure was a huge disappointment to her. I am sure that she must have felt that I had thrown cold water on a burning piece of metal. She must have thought that I was a total *nurd*, but I did what seemed to be the right thing to do at the moment. Obviously, I had to avoid future encounters with Pam in order to not be tempted again.

The unfortunate incident destroyed our friendship, and I was never able to apologize or explain my actions. I felt like a *heel*. Being married, I could not talk to my friends about what went wrong. I had no intention of hurting her. Her invaluable friendship, love, and tutoring were so instrumental in my obtaining my master's degree, which I accomplished in 1969.

Shortly thereafter I began studies for my doctoral program at the University of Northern Colorado in Greeley and later at Denver University.

Lack of finances, political pressures from Iran, and my troubled home life did not allow me to complete these studies.

I accepted a teaching position in Longmont, Colorado to take advantage of the practical training it afforded me and to remain in the U.S. per immigration laws. Foreign students were permitted to work eighteen months after each degree earned in America. Longmont, of which I have many fond memories, became my first permanent home in the United States. The birth of my second daughter, Eli, was a highlight, but unfortunately Hava's and my marriage ended there.

My struggle with the English language continued for a long time. The first year of my teaching in a public junior high school provided its own set of challenges. As part of my duties, I was assigned to monitor hallways, showers, and bathrooms. For natives familiar with the system and the culture it would not have been *a big deal.* For me it was a disaster! With no information to prepare myself and to learn about the new duties, especially in the bathroom, my job turned out to be a *dandy* one. I was embarrassed to ask the principal or other faculty members for help. I was very proud of my teaching capabilities and did not wish to *damage my pride* or my image by admitting that as an Iranian I was unable to perform a simple task in my new position. Thus, it became a *pain you know where.*

I reviewed all my college notes, searched through every class textbook in the graduate program, but none of these sources provided information for this specific duty. I knew my undergraduate books would not be of any help because we did not have bathroom duty in Iran.

One day, I was in the boys' restroom, standing around like a *weirdo*, not knowing what I was supposed to do or look for. Was I expected to be sure no one *pissed* on the floor or was it my job to check and see if their pants were zipped up all the way? It even crossed my mind that maybe not wasting toilet paper was the reason for a teacher to be there! Perhaps they wanted me to be there to check that everyone flushed the toilets! Whatever their reasons were, I could not figure the *darn thing out*. Often I felt the students looked at me rather strangely as if thinking, what is this weird man doing here?

Growing up in Iran, privacy and modesty were part of our lives. Before coming to America, I had never experienced a group shower where everyone marched around naked, and especially in front of their teachers or students. Even with my close friends and teammates in public baths people were expected to cover their private parts. Each customer upon arrival would be handed a dark red cloth called, "loneg" to wrap around his waist while walking in front of the others. Thus, under these new and surprising restroom circumstances, I must say it shocked me to a point that I had no desire to be there at all. I needed time to get used to the change; yet, I was expected to "supervise."

To make matters worse, on my third day a student came to me saying, in a complaining tone of voice, that John *flipped a birdie* at him. I asked the boy, "What kind and color was she?" meaning the bird. "Was she pretty?" He looked at me totally disturbed for a minute and then started running away.

I did not know what I had said wrong to the poor boy. This made me *mumble to myself* in the teacher's lounge afterward, trying to figure out what I said that made him look at me so strangely. Several colleagues noticed my discomfort and offered their help. After a brief explanation, one teacher suggested that if I could repeat the conversation to the best of my memory, she might be able to assist. I did and suddenly everyone was laughing. After that incident my colleagues nicknamed me "The Bird."

Now, with over three and a half decades of studying and practicing English in America, I am still not quite sure if I *get it*. Recently a friend of mine introduced her best friend saying, "Lisa is full of *piss and vinegar*!" I didn't know what to say or how to respond since I had never heard that expression.

The word screw *screwed me up*. I did not know how a small construction item can be used in so many different contexts: *John is a screw ball, Shirley is a screwed up mess, don't screw with me, buster* and *I got screwed at the car dealership yesterday*! How can a foreigner make sense out of these?

I anonymously received this rhyme by e-mail and thought that it echoed my thoughts about the English language.

THE CRAZIEST LANGUAGE

We'll begin with a box and the plural is boxes
But the plural of ox is oxen and not oxes.
Then, one fowl is a goose, but two are called geese,
Yet the plural of moose should never be meese.
You may find a lone mouse or nest full of mice,
Yet the plural of house is houses, not hice.
If the plural of man is always called men:
Why shouldn't the plural of pan be called pen?
If I spoke of my foot and show you my feet,
And I gave you a boot, would a pair be called beet?
If one is a tooth and a whole set are called teeth,
Why shouldn't the plural of booth be called beeth?
Then one may be that, and three would be those,
Yet hat in the plural would never be hose,
And the plural of cat is cats, not cose.
We speak of a brother and also of brethren,
But although we say mother, we never say methren.
Then the masculine pronouns are he, his and him,
But imagine the feminine, she, shis and shim.
So English I fancy and you will agree:
Is the craziest language you ever did see.

169

To close this chapter on a happy note and to exemplify the universal struggle with communication, I include a letter that a friend gave me during my first year in Wyoming. He wanted to warn and prepare me for my future linguistic misunderstandings and the many complications that commonly ensue!

"There was a little old lady school teacher looking for a room in Switzerland. She asked the local village school-master to help her. A place that suited her was found and she returned to London for her luggage. She remembered she had not noticed a bathroom, or as she called it, a water closet. She wrote the schoolmaster and asked whether or not there was a WC in or near the house. The schoolmaster, who did not know the English expression, was puzzled by the WC, never dreaming she was talking about a bathroom. He finally sought the parish priest's advice, and they concluded that WC must mean Wayside Chapel. The lady received the following letter a few days later:

Dear Madame:

The WC is located 9 miles from the house in the heart of a beautiful grove of trees. It will seat 350 people at one time and is open on Tuesday, Thursday and Sunday each week. Some people like to take their lunch and make a day out of it. Thursday there is organ accompaniment. The acoustics are very good and the slightest sound can be heard by everyone. It may interest you to know that my daughter met her husband at the W.C. We are now in the process of taking donations to purchase plush seats. We feel this is a long-felt need, since the present seats have holes in them. My wife is rather delicate; therefore, she hasn't been able to attend regularly. It has been six months since she last went. Naturally it pains her very much not to be able to go more often. I will close now with the desire to accommodate you in every way possible and will be happy to save you a seat either down front or near the door, whichever you prefer."

I taught and coached in Vail from 1980 until my retirement in 1995 with outstanding principals, staff, parents, and students. Words cannot begin to describe the faculty's superb personalities combined with their teaching qualifications. They made me feel at home and the entire supportive community expressed appreciation for my contribution to their children's successes. Living in a first-class resort, skiing, and working with a group of wonderful colleagues for many years, was an experience I will cherish for the rest of my life.

Today I feel fortunate to be considered one of many professionals born in a different country, who are respected for who they are and what they have accomplished in their new country.

As a teacher it has always been my intent to encourage and inspire students beyond what they may think is possible to achieve. As a lecturer in schools, colleges, clubs, and cruise lines, I strive to excite and stimulate my audiences. I am proud to think that I am able to do this in a second language with an acceptable degree of success.

Perhaps this is the time to thank each and every one of my wonderful American friends who helped me establish my roots in new soil. Special gratitude is owed to my outstanding college instructors who granted me extra time in completing tests. My admiration goes to the wonderful teachers who allowed me to take oral examinations so that my lack of English comprehension would not be a hindrance to my grades. Thanks also to the secretaries and friends who typed my term papers and thesis, to the bankers who trusted me enough to lend me money in critical times, to the principals and deans who hired me based on my qualifications and did not discriminate because of my place of birth.

I will forever feel indebted to them all and will always have a special place in my heart for them. I admire their great sense of humanity.

I also would like to express my gratitude to everyone who helped me to reach the finish line in that long and hard journey. I hope that they will accept my apologies when I was not able to give them more in return at the time. I did not have anything to offer. They all were the greatest. My thanks go to the sincere parents who trusted me to teach, coach, and develop their children's potential. Helping my students to become district, state, national champions or obtain scholarships at universities was my highest accomplishment. Their success was the best reward for me.

The author at the World University Games in Sofia, Bulgaria, 1961 with Igor Ter-Ovanesian of Russia, 1960 and 1964 Olympic Medalist in the long jump

HOW LONG DOES IT TAKE?

In addition to my own experiences in assimilating to a new culture, I have for the past two decades conversed and questioned other immigrants and their families who reside in the United States, Europe, and Canada. I have been intrigued by the process of assimilation, such as, the length of time it takes a person to actually integrate from one culture into another. In other words, "How long and what does it take for a person to be able to take root again and begin growing in a new soil, a question broached in the opening statement of this book." For this research I did not find a definite time framework nor did I see a specific set of guidelines for such a process; however, after generalizing my findings, I came up with the following conclusions:

One, it definitely takes more than five years;

Two, it requires an enormous amount of patience and perseverance; and

Three, it is a huge undertaking.

Language seems to be the biggest barrier. Some of the older immigrants feel almost as if they are under "house arrest" in that they cannot communicate or read in the new language and feel extremely awkward in public places. Those in their 20's, 30's, and 40's are at times embarrassed because of many linguistic misunderstandings which create problems in their social and professional lives. Many teenagers easily learn the new language and adapt to a new life style. Others find not only the usual trials and tribulations of being a teenager difficult, but are overwhelmed by the added burden of trying to be accepted, let alone assimilate. The young children are the ones who learn a second language the quickest without major problems.

Language aside, there are many other obstacles to overcome, such as different family values, social mores, religion, foods, music, and entertainment. Intermarriage can facilitate the absorption of different cultures into the main

173

cultural body; however, it often takes three generations for an immigrant family to fully become accepted.

I visited many immigrant families on a regular basis to observe up close and in person their adaptation to a new lifestyle. My questions were asked casually and informally in order to avoid putting anyone under any pressure. I purposely did not take notes in their presence nor did I use a tape recorder. The subject families were most commonly not aware of my research for this book; therefore, their responses came from the heart and without reservation.

Surprisingly, their issues were quite similar. In fact, their concerns were so much and so frequently the same that had I not known each family well, I would have thought that by mistake I had been conversing with the same people.

They shared identical problems in trying to adapt to their new language, the food, customs, music, social behavior, etc. as reasons for a common unhappiness. Whether they were political refugees who ran for their lives and had to accept whichever country would take them, or whether they independently chose their new country and new life, many seemed discontented.

The cultural parameters of a new country and/or new life expand beyond immigrants merely moving from one nation to another. It also includes all those who have experienced a dramatic political change within their own country. In the same way, the latter have to adapt and adjust at multiple levels in order to learn to fit in and be accepted in their new society.

For example, in 1979 in Iran, the Islamic Revolution created a politically and socially new country for its citizens which in turn forced a sudden and drastic change of lifestyle propelling them centuries backwards in a single day. The women, perhaps, felt it the most as they were forced to abandon more modern attire and cover themselves from head to toe with the *chador,* wear no make-up, and sit at the back of the bus. They were segregated from the men in public places, such as restaurants, movies, beaches, and swimming pools, and only were allowed to be in such places if they had a male escort. At the beaches and swimming pools, the women had to be fully clothed with heads covered when they went into the water. For many educated females who held important jobs and were used to wearing the latest fashions from Paris, London, and Milan, this social repression and isolation robbed them of all sense of well being and self worth.

Men were also obligated to accept this completely different lifestyle. No longer could they show affection to their wives or fiancees in public places. They, too, felt isolated and repressed. Imagine going on a honeymoon and not being able to enjoy a few of simple pleasures of being together, such as holding hands during a walk in the park, taking a midnight swim, sitting next to each other in a movie theater, or a spontaneous affectionate hug at a restaurant.

For years, women were not allowed to attend a soccer match held in Tehran's stadium, because they would, naturally, be surrounded by men in the stands and would be watching the players clad in shorts. This created much frustration which all came to a head in 1998 at the World Cup final qualifying game against the Hungarian team. Thousands of suppressed women rebelled and burst through the stadium doors to gain access to the game. This bold action, which was totally against the Ayatollah's personal interpretation of already restrictive Islamic rules, surprised and befuddled the mullahs and government officials. It was a victory for the women of Iran, because ever since that day, they have been permitted to watch soccer and any other sporting events along with their male counterparts.

Other examples are the former communist nations which are now newly independent, many with new names, borders, and with governments dictating a totally different lifestyle. If not observant, one might think that life is the same or even better for these people, not necessarily so. For those citizens who were not educated and mentally ready, the radical changes instituted enormous emotional hardships. It is not easy to accept a sudden change of lifestyle without at least some prior preparation.

While visiting the Czech Republic in the spring of 1996, I observed that many of the fields lay barren. When I questioned the tour director as to why, he explained that under the communist regime, citizens were trained to be "single task" individuals. All a farmer needed to do was plant, grow, harvest, pick, pack, and put his crates next to the road. It was not his responsibility to do anything more. Another "single task" individual would transport the product to the markets in the nation. Purchasing tractors, repairing them, paying for related expenses, bookkeeping, shipping, balancing income and expenses, profit projections, marketing, budgeting, and paying employees were taken care of by the state. A farmer did not have to worry about medical expenses for himself or his family, and his children's future and education were not a concern to him, as everything was taken care of by the government.

Under the new democratic and capitalist government, a small parcel of land was given to each farmer. This ownership, instead of making him independent or prosperous, created disaster as he had not been trained to handle the multiple facets of free enterprise and had no understanding of the concept of profit or loss, hiring and firing, or other needed knowledge of entrepreneurship. Successful farming operations now required a knowledge of marketing, selling, financing, and being responsible for the entire business which he did not have. As a result, most farmers were not working and consequently starving. Sadly, for many of these families stealing, selling drugs, teenage prostitution, and working in the black market became a way of survival.

President Bush, with his massive military attack on Iraq in March 2003, pretentiously stated that he was liberating the people by removing Saddam Hussein and making Iraq "democratic." But in reality, he has made daily life for the Iraqis more miserable than before. Already some sixty percent of the population was incapable of feeding itself, and it was

Saddam and his government who delivered bread to them to avoid starvation.

It is true that Saddam was a tyrant, a criminal, and a merciless killer. But he is not the only inhuman leader on this planet. There are at least twelve other leaders and their governments who are as barbaric. Why Saddam Hussein was singled out remains a big question in many people's minds.

President Bush and his staff seem to be ignorant of or exhibit a fundamental lack of understanding of Iraq, the Middle East, and the Moslem faith and culture. The vast majority of Iraq's population, which feared and hated Saddam, equally hate and fear American presence and occupation of their land. The 1991 Persian Gulf War is still fresh in their minds where a "successful mission" for the American military was killing Iraqis or destroying electrical plants, telephone lines, bridges, highways, factories, sewage facilities, dams, schools and hospitals by dropping some 88,500 tons of bombs on Iraq. We subsequently promised to militarily help both the Kurds in the north and the Shi'a moslems in the south if they revolted against Saddam. For whatever reasons, we did not keep our promise. The sad consequence was that Saddam retaliated against these people with chemical warfare, and thousands were gassed to death. But this was not the only time Saddam used chemical weapons. He had done the same against the Iranians in the 1980's. Ironically, little mention has been made of this and it did not upset us. This U.S. takeover of Iraq will prove to be very costly in regard to human losses, to both Americans and Iraqis, as well as becoming an enormous financial burden to our nation.

President Bush says that he wants Iraq to be a beacon of democracy in the Middle East, but first there must be peace, and peace does not come with tanks, missiles, bombs and B-52s. Peace and democracy can only be achieved through diplomacy and education. War is not a solution for economic, social or political problems. We need to bridge the gulf between the West and the Middle East by educating people how to

177

resolve their differences and conflicts in a diplomatic manner and by instilling respect, tolerance, appreciation, and understanding for all the people of the world.

Abrupt and radical changes of their government, culture, customs and life style will take time, perhaps generations, for many Iraqis to adapt to and understand. Is the U.S. willing and prepared to help in this long process?

Name calling, such as the "Axis of Evil," "Evil Doers", and propagating the myth of the "civilized world" versus the "uncivilized world" is not helpful and only exacerbates the problem.

President Bush's plan for "democratization" has made Iraqis face an even more uncertain, wretched life because of the looting, crime, and lawlessness. In addition to not having electricity, safe drinking water, or a steady income Iraqis are experiencing serious other problems. According to a German reporter representing the United Nations thousands of Iraqi children have died or are dying throughout the course of these wars due to contaminated water.

During the course of my research, I found that in general the age of individuals experiencing a change in lifestyle is an extremely significant factor in determining the length of time it takes to adjust, assimilate, and to change one's former way of thinking to a new one. The younger they were, the shorter period it took to adjust and blend into a new life. Infants did not need any time at all, unless they were raised in a family who only spoke their native language at home and maintained their old culture to the detriment of the new. Speech was the most noticeable handicap for immigrant children. Instead of communicating at the normal, expected time frame for their age group, they took a year or two longer. Needless to say, parents worried that their babies had a learning disability. They were unaware of the complicated process that their child had to go through to learn to speak, let alone, understand and respond in two different languages, especially in school.

For Iranian children in America, the double input of English spoken around them and Farsi at home was confusing. However, the amazing fact is that when these children began to speak, they proved to be bilingual. Those parents who were conscious of the complicated process and subsequent linguistic delay often purposely avoided speaking their native language at home. Speaking only one language at home helped the children in communicating in the new language at an earlier age, but it ironically caused them to miss an opportunity to maintain their native language and the option of a second language for later use in life.

Elementary-age children needed a very short time to adjust. The school environment and their playmates helped them to think, act, and grow up American. I remember our first year in the United States when we did not have a Christmas tree at home to celebrate the occasion as we were unfamiliar with this custom. Our two-and-a-half year old daughter Sima cried for a long time, asking us why Santa Claus did not come to our house to leave her presents while he delivered gifts to all her friends in the neighborhood. The abundant commercialization of Christmas on television and everywhere else added to her confusion and sadness as well. We could not convince her with our logic and eventually had to buy a tree for her the next year and years thereafter. Naturally we also placed a few presents under the tree. She liked this new tradition very much and now that she is a mature adult she has made sure that it continues!

The adjustment for high school adolescents was quite difficult for both the teenagers and their parents. Of course, it varied depending on their place of birth, religion, and culture. If the parents accepted the new way of life and the freedom of lifestyle allowed in the new country given to them, it made it easier for their teenagers; but often this was not the case. The kids wanted the freedoms their friends and peers had. The easy-going lifestyle, the dress code or lack thereof, and the possibility of sexual encounters enticed and excited them immensely. Simultaneously, they were frustrated by the strict rules and opposition they received at home.

Dating, flirting, casual sex, wild parties, drugs and alcohol were all forbidden to these immigrant teenagers who came from Moslem countries. In good conscience, they could not participate in such "fun" activities because of parental pressure or their own cultural differences and traditions. If they were attracted to someone, they could not express their feelings in the same way their classmates did, which ironically placed them in an awkward social position in school and society. The traditional restrictions imposed on them in turn created many misunderstandings and hardships within the family itself. The youth wanted to embrace the new life and did not like being suffocated in the old traditions, regardless of the possible deterioration of their relationships with their parents.

Ponytails for boys, body piercing, dread locks, orange hair, and black lipstick offended and hurt the old-fashioned Moslem parents deeply. Hearing their child's rude response to their pleas often was enough to cause seizures or heart attacks. "It's a free country; I can do whatever I want," was a pierced arrow in many parents' hearts. Premarital sex and/or marrying without parental approval unthought of in the old country, caused many unforgivable humiliations. Many parents were heartbroken because culturally they could not cope with the lack of respect and consideration their children showed them.

It is hard for me to forget a sarcastic remark an Iranian-Canadian father made in regard to his pregnant daughter getting married. He said, "She was four months pregnant when her boyfriend came to me to ask for her hand in marriage." I told the young man, " Why are you asking for my daughter's hand from me now, when you have had everything else!"

Immigrant sons and daughters not taking advantage of the abundant educational opportunities and possibilities available in America and Europe for a better future created additional stress and anguish. A very good friend of mine who lived in Amsterdam shared her disappointment with me. Her son had been accepted to a local college, but he refused to pursue it. He had absolutely no ambition or desire to make something of himself. I was sympathetic, knowing how upsetting it was to lose the dream she had for her son's future. She had left everything behind in Iran after the Islamic takeover in hopes of protecting her family and offering her two children a much better life. Her heroic escape, hiding in bathrooms in trains, and the terror she experienced at the thought of being caught with the wrong traveling documents, still were vivid images for her.

Her 24-year-old son disregarded the sacrifices she had made and the suffering she had endured by preferring to stay at home, sleeping until noon, and "meditating" for the rest of the day. As a highly motivated, determined, directional mother, she could not understand such thinking.

My talented daughter Eli, who received her master's degree with a full grant, was hired by her university as head lab technician, an accomplishment which made me very proud. However, while I was lecturing on a cruise ship sailing to Sydney, Australia she e-mailed that she could not wait to tell me about her new career, but she had to tell me in person. I was so excited thinking that she had received another grant to pursue her doctoral program or had been offered a dream job at another university. I could not sleep for days with anxious anticipation and joy. The first thing I did upon arrival at the airport was to call her. Her big news was that she was going to resign from the university to play a banjo and sing in a local band! Without thinking, I responded, "Don't give up your daytime job until you become famous enough to support me!" Even though she has a great voice and talent, which may make her successful, fortunately she for once listened to me and also kept her job. On August 30th, 2003 she married a wonderful young man she loves, and they have started a very happy life together, which is the biggest reward for me.

Many such youthful decisions regarding marriage and career were unheard of in the old culture. Most children even as adults, would ask for their father's opinion concerning a career and respect his ideas for choosing the most prosperous future.

After living in America for a few years, the new found

freedom and equality caused some Moslem wives to demonstrate sudden and dramatic personality changes. Often they misinterpreted the women's liberation movement and instead of educating and bettering themselves, they became revengeful and spiteful. They became bitter and retaliated against their spouses for an ancient cultural rule which the husbands had nothing to do with. Many were intelligent, educated men who tried to provide for and take care of their wives and families in the traditional way.

With changes in some women's attitudes came numerous demands that turned family life upside-down. Many cases resulted in the dissolution of marriages, causing entire families to suffer with resultant negative effects that went far beyond what they had bargained for.

I sincerely hope that the reader will not interpret my logic as that of a chauvinistic male, not giving proper consideration to women's rights. I have the highest admiration for my present American wife, in every aspect. She trusts my judgment in business dealings without arguing over every little item. But out of the love and respect I have for her ideas and contributions to our happy family life, I personally would not make a major decision without consulting her. I must confess also that I had no respect for my father, a useless drunk who abused his wives and children, nor for my grandfather who had three spouses. My hero throughout my life has been a woman, my grandmother. She was petite and never demanded or raised her voice with anyone. She acted bigger and was more effective than any prestigious, strong man I know.

The unreasonable pressures and requests by the wives of their husbands only punished the innocent spouse, did not/does not change the Islamic mandate, and only destroyed/destroys many families.

Life in many cases became chaotic when spouses began demanding to be equal partners in business without prior expertise. Those women who obtained a basic, fundamental education or went through on-the-job training and acquired the

182

necessary business skills did a great job. But 90 percent of such spouses did not admit their lack of knowledge or experience; they just wanted to be boss. Needless to say, a large number of these businesses had irreparable monetary losses.

Through the years of gathering information for this book, I have witnessed many so-called husband and wife partnerships collapse. Financial losses were the main reasons for "killing the root in the new soil." The overall long-term negative effects of the losses on families was devastating.

As for my personal experiences in America, my first wife Hava ordered me to share the household duties. Although I worked four jobs, and she sat all day at home watching soap operas, I was expected to cook, clean, wash dishes, and do laundry when I came home exhausted. I normally worked 80 hours or more per week to make the payments for the house, car, insurance, schooling, and medical expenses while she complained about not being treated fairly if I did not do my share of the housework. I can well remember coming home at 9:00 p.m. worn-out and asking what there was for dinner? Her tart reply was, "It's your turn to cook."

I would have understood had she said that she too was tired, had too many things to do, didn't feel like cooking, or wanted to eat out. But no, she just wanted to make it clear to me that I would not label her housekeeper or cook. Because of my involvement in the community, most people in town knew me, and when introducing her as my wife, she would be enraged. She forcefully said: "I am Hava, and would appreciate not being referred to as Parviz's wife."

Once I came home to the startling news that she wanted to look for a job. I was pleased to hear it since the majority of Iranian wives traditionally did not work outside the home. I thought it would do wonders for her to get out and meet people. She must have found staying home boring. So, in support of her idea, I wanted to please her and do my best to help. Immediately I tried to call a few people I knew to find a baby-sitter so Hava would be free to pursue her wish. She

183

grabbed the phone out of my hand, telling me, "A baby-sitter won't do, you must stay home tomorrow with Sima, as it is your turn." It was an impossible demand. I could not call the school district to tell them that I could not teach because my wife would not permit me to come to work. Furthermore, had they agreed, it would have been a day off without pay. Teaching was my full-time job; I also had several part-time jobs and graduate school. However, no other alternative was acceptable to Hava.

With her newfound freedom she became malicious, and used the American legal system to hurt and punish me. Some years later, we separated and later divorced. Hava did not believe in joint custody of our children. I had just as much parental right to our children as she did, but she made sure, by extraordinary insistence and paying substantial amounts of money to her numerous attorneys, that my daughters would be taken away from me. Her legal battles cost me an astronomical amount of money for attorney's fees. But their fees were nothing in comparison to the pain I suffered in not seeing my daughters grow up. My sole role as a father was to mail a monthly child support check.

Perversely, many young adults, after graduating from high school or college, learned to take advantage of both cultures. When they should have been listening to mature parental advice, they cleverly did what they wanted and defended their rights gained by living in a free country. However, in times of need, such as a purchase of a car or paying off credit cards, they became masters at pretending to be respectful, obedient, loving children who valued parental guidance, and therefore were automatically entitled to gifts of money by virtue of being perfect. It amazed me to observe how well some had convinced their parents to celebrate both Moslem and Christian holidays to receive twice the presents they would be showered with otherwise. If only they could have convinced their parents to celebrate Hanukkah, it would have made them even happier!

Senior citizens had the hardest time adjusting, as they

needed a much longer period to establish "strong roots" in the new country. Some didn't even come close to accepting, learning, or understanding their new culture. Nothing resembled life as they knew it before. Even the absence of the traditional tea houses in the neighborhood created loneliness in their lives. The male members no longer had a place to smoke their *hookah*, a special pipe for smoking with a long flexible tube which draws the smoke through water in a vase, and sit around chatting with their companions for hours on end. They could not socialize, meet friends, sip a cup of strong brewed tea, exchange news, catch up on gossip or play a pleasant game of backgammon. These century-old tea houses had been an integral part of their daily life. Modern, bustling coffee shops with a hundred varieties of teas, coffees, cappuccinos, and cafe lattes never replaced that traditional cup of strong, steamed black tea.

Learning a second language became next to impossible, which made their feelings of isolation even more acute. I have seen many old timers become depressed and frustrated in their new countries because they could not communicate with others in their native language. Everyone was expected to know and accept the "new" language as being the only one.

The segment of the population that I studied most was the middle-aged parents with children who were born in Iran. Their problems of making a happy new life stemmed from their impractical way of thinking which seemed quite unrealistic to me. Many had a hard time accepting where the present situation in Iran, one of economic hardship, political repression, and stifling Islamic conservatism, was heading. They thought of it as just another gray period in Iran's history that would soon be over, and they would shortly return to their homeland taking their newfound freedom and beliefs with them. Others, who had no desire to return, spoke starry-eyed of transporting their luxurious homes from Iran to their present place of residence. My American wife and I would often give each other a surprised and quizzical look whenever we heard these foolish, outlandish statements. We were curious to know how they possibly thought that they were going to cart their homes from Iran to Amsterdam, Paris, London, New York or Los Angeles!

Some were depressed because they couldn't afford to have servants in their new country. The women lamented and wondered how they would be able to survive without their maids! None of them could understand why menial labor cost so much in Western countries, especially America. Without the material wealth and success they had been accustomed to in the old country, most felt like they were poverty stricken in their new country. This loss of prosperity and status made the majority miserable.

Hardly any of them felt comfortable with, nor did they express interest in, meeting and associating with people of their newly adopted nation. Instead they gathered with their fellow Iranians to celebrate their own special events including *No Rooz*, the Persian New Year. They protectively isolated themselves in their own private world, establishing various cultural, educational, religious, musical and artistic societies for performances and exhibitions. This is somewhat similar to many U.S. servicemen and their families overseas who spend their entire tour of duty on base fraternizing with other Americans at their private clubs, bowling alley and theater, never interacting or learning the language of the host country, except to order a single meal or a beer.

Most people from the Middle East who moved to Europe were less than happy because of the small apartments given to them by the government. They felt smothered and shackled. Many hoped eventually to be able to immigrate to America, the imagined land of wide open spaces, unlimited opportunities, and wealth. Their wishful thinking of an easy life in the United States amused me. I tried to convince them that they would be better off making the best of what they already had rather than wasting their time fantasizing. I had little to no luck in our conversations in trying to make them realize that they probably could not afford a comprehensive health insurance premium in America, let alone expect a much better life. In my opinion,

186

living in the past and day dreaming of a fantasy future made most of the people I studied forget about a much needed commitment to the here and now. As a consequence, they could never enjoy nor improve what they had in order to become happy.

My not vacillating back and forth has led me in one direction only, forward. I am proud to be an American and very happy to live here. It took me seven years to make my decision, but after I did, I made the very best of it and have no regrets. In contrast, I know a sizable number of so-called "hopeless" immigrants who have separated themselves from any possibility of having a successful personal or professional life.

I asked three questions of everyone to understand their position in this crucial transition. *"Where is your mind, where is your heart, and where is your life?"* I was stunned by not hearing one single reply that indicated acceptance of or fitting into their new culture. One Polish friend said her mind is in Germany, her heart is in Poland, and her home is in America. This meant she really did not want to be here. I believe that kind of thinking, based on an impossible dream, places all of these immigrants in a miserable and inescapable position. It takes away their chances of happiness *right off the bat*.

To me, there was always one answer. "My mind is in building and creating, my heart is in sharing, giving and making the best out of what I have and where I was, and my home is in the country I chose to live in. In reality, I feel that I am a citizen of the world." It is my wish to see all the people who live in a new country consider it their home instead of placing undue importance on the country from which they come. Whether you are a Jew, an Arab, or a Chinese, I strongly believe that you must place your priority with the country where you are living. Definitely, this would eliminate some of the enormous problems being faced in America.

In these recent times, a special group merits particular attention, those of Islamic heritage. The vast majority of these latter came to America wanting to embrace their new country but have had to face additional challenges and obstacles. The two most common are:

1. Being labeled "terrorist,"a stigma given to them by the media and unfair, sensational tabloids.

2. Personal family conflicts as a direct result of cultural differences.

In addition, some have created their own hardships by misusing freedom in America and further complicated life for themselves and others by taking unfair advantage of the legal system. They have learned the tricks in filing fabricated lawsuits and making false claims with the hope of making easy money. In the process they have caused self-destruction as well as grief and suffering for all involved.

For the past 20 years politicians and the news media have misled the American public into having a negative attitude toward Moslems. Unfortunately, the heinous 9/11 act of terror in America, brought about by a group of fanatics from Saudi Arabia reinforced and created more hatred and fear among Americans in this unfounded hatred for Moslems. The slur of "terrorist" has affected and tainted the lives of Moslem immigrants who live in the United States and other western countries. The fact is that out of 1.6 billion Moslems in the world one percent are classified as Fundamentalists who engage in acts of terror and destruction against America and other countries perceived to be in allegiance with America. President Bush's unjustified attack on Iraq, killing many innocent people in the process has not helped the situation as it has created many baby Bin Ladens for the future. These new terrorists do not need to be a member of Al-Qaeda or other anti-American organizations seeking retribution as they would act on their own simply because of being possibly orphaned, suffering loss of home and all family possessions, or surviving day to day in barbaric conditions. They have absolutely nothing to lose and no hope for a future all of which makes these individuals irrational and volatile.

Ninety-nine percent of Moslems are decent, religious human beings, but because of being ostracized, many of them residing in foreign countries prefer not to mention their place of birth or religion, avoiding the unpleasant feeling of being excluded. This explains why many Iranians abroad prefer to say they are from Persia, the old name for Iran, and that they are Persians, in hopes that no one will connect the two.

Many Americans have shown in their conversations with me an astonishing lack of knowledge in geography. Some did not have the slightest idea where Persia was. A few "smart" understanding ones shook their heads and politely said, "How nice!" Some have asked if I meant Prussia. At times when I said that I was from Iran, they thought I meant Iraq and kept asking me questions about Saddam Hussein which I thought was quite amusing.

No one appreciates being discriminated against based on his place of birth or for whatever reason. When my American wife was falling in love with me, her excited happy face made her family, colleagues, and friends curious to ask her for more information about me. She told them I was an educator and a wonderful person with whom she had much in common. As my name was not a familiar American name, they then asked where I was from. Her reply, "the Middle East" made their mouths fall open in astonishment. Some even had the audacity to say, "You are not serious, are you? How can you think of marrying a terrorist?" This was 1990 and the prejudice has increased since 9/11/2001.

ازانتصاب رئیس جدید تربیت بدنی اظهارخشنودی کردند

درج و منتشر میسازد و باینوسیله
موجبات تشویق جوانان‌ورزشکاران‌را
فراهم می آورد ، از انتصاب آقای
افتخار زاده بریاست قریب بعفی
خرمشهر اظهار خشنودی کردند.
باید دانست ، آقای افتخار زاده
ازطرف آقای مهندس حکیمی‌رئیس
فرهنگ خرمشهر باین سمت منصوب
شده و این حسن انتصاب موجب
خشنودی کلیه ورزشکاران این شهر
گردیده است .
آقای فیروز افتخار زاده فارغ
التحصیل رشته تربیت بدنی‌دانش‌
سرایعالی است و تابحال جزوتیم
های ورزشی و پیشاهنگی به‌کشور
های انگلستان ، ترکیه ، فرانسه ،
آلمان ، بلژیک ،اتریش ،بلغارستان
ویوگسلاوی مسافرت کردهومسابقات
مهمی بهمربانان این‌ کشور ها
انجام داده است . همچنین وکدو
سال قبل از طرف دانشگاه‌تهران
برای شرکت در مسابقات دوومیدانی
دانشجویان که در صوبه برگزار

خبرنگار ما در خرمشهر طی
گزارشی مینویسد :چند روز قبل
عده‌ای از روسای باشگاه‌ ها و
نمایندگان ورزشکاران خرمشهر
بدفتر نمایندگی اطلاعات در این
شهرستان آمدند و ضمن اظهار
تشکر از روزنامه اطلاعات که اخبار
ورزشی شهرستانها را در اسرع‌وقت

دراین شماره از

اهواز
خرمشهر
خرم‌آباد
شوشتر
مسجدسلیمان

آقای فیروز افتخار زاده

شده صوبه اعزام‌گردیدواشیازات
قابل توجهی در مسابقات مذکور
بدست آورد ودرهمان سال بدریافت
چندین‌نشان ورزشی‌زمستخشاهنشاه
مفتخر گردید .

Ettela-ot newspaper article describing author's
position and accomplishments in Khoramshahr, Iran

190

THE SEEMINGLY IMPOSSIBLE
TAKES A LITTLE LONGER

In 1976 while teaching full time, I dreamt of building an athletic club. I designed some preliminary plans which included a projection of predicted income and expenses. Then I searched for investors. My innovative project attracted my brother plus eight other close friends to invest in it. Full of excitement, I diligently started looking for a construction loan. I went to 36 banks and lending institutions across the state and was turned down by all of them.

My efforts and absorption in building the athletic club became the main issue of contention in our marriage, eventually leading to irreconcilable differences and the dissolution of our marriage. Hava was eminently against the idea, strongly believing that I had lost my mind and my sense of reality in wanting to start such a large scale investment, especially as my first business enterprise in America. She was convinced that my dream could only happen through a major miracle.

After a series of daily arguments and threats, she gave me her last ultimatum: "What is so hard for you to understand that this crazy dream of yours is not possible? You don't have the money and I do not see your rich daddy helping you out by putting up the cash you need. Where will you find such a large amount of money to build your silly, expensive club?" Then she continued, "Because of your stupid idea, my life, and that of our children, is miserable." Hava offered me two choices: one, to see a psychiatrist in Boulder or Denver; the other, to open a restaurant. She said that she would give me her full support if I would also agree to make her older brother, who arrived last week *fresh* from Iran and did not speak a word of English, the manager and the bartender! That was her best offer. She made it quite clear that if I didn't agree to set up an appointment with a therapist, or commit to open a restaurant, our marriage was over.

I begged Hava to be patient with me for three more months as I knew we were so close to reaching our goal. I could envision the club, with the parking lot full of cars, and people playing tennis on the outdoor courts every time I stood on the property. I also mentioned the benefits that our family would receive from this investment if she just would stand by me. I even told Hava that I would sleep on the couch and promised to make up to her and our children for any inconveniences or sacrifices they would have to make if she would only give me enough time to secure a loan.

It was out of the question as Hava did not want to hear any more about it. She did not want to negotiate or compromise. It had to be her way or no way. Without any apparent sense of compassion, she immediately wanted to file for a divorce. My repeated requests to think about what she was doing, destroying our family life, and cautionary words as to the adverse effects her filing might have on my being approved for a loan, did not change her mind. Without hesitation she told me: "I don't care." To leave my daughters was the last thing in the world I ever expected to do and to pack my clothes and walk out of my home devastated me.

In the 1970s athletic clubs were not the *rage* they are now, and, to be sure conservative farm towns like Longmont, did not have loan officers interested in financing a health club. To ask for a farm or tractor loan was no problem, but most laughed at my futuristic proposal to build a health facility in the community. I did not let their rejections dissuade me, because I have never taken "no" for an answer.

Fortunately, the 37th financial institution, First National Bank of Ft. Collins, approved my loan, guaranteed by the Small Business Administration. A short time afterwards, construction began and within six months the club was a reality. With the initial investment and a permanent loan of $350,000 my dream of a modern, private, athletic facility was realized when we opened in 1978 in Longmont, Colorado. It included a large gymnasium designed to accommodate the four hundred twenty gymnastic students enrolled in my program. It also had workout rooms with the latest equipment, racquetball and squash courts, tennis courts, a swimming pool, pro shop, snack bar, indoor and outdoor running tracks, and more. We didn't lack for members, and the athletic club was a very popular place.

We owned five and a half acres of prime commercial real estate in a central location in town which made the club and its land a valuable investment, capable of many future expansions. Our quick success made some locals envious, specifically a jealous banker with whom we dealt, as the initial loan from First National Bank of Ft. Collins was transferred to his bank in Longmont. He befriended my brother Ray and Mohammed (Mo), a colleague of my brother from Iran who was the second major shareholder after Ray. The banker persuaded them to fire me and hire another manager at a lower salary. Trusting him, my brother and Mo followed his advice in hopes of a better return on their investments. He also instructed Ray and Mo to set higher salaries for themselves. The insidious banker's influence and intervention ended up destroying our partnership, our friendship, and a better return on our investment.

In my absence, it was not long before the club began to experience a rapid decline in both membership and money. The anticipated steady projected income gradually faded away. As I had been dismissed in the middle of the school year, I could not find a replacement teaching or coaching position or any job whatsoever. This moment had to be the lowest point of my life, without my daughters, alone, and unemployed. My heavy-heartedness, brought about by devoting years of hard work, but not being able to realize my dream, absolutely ripped me apart. The stress was almost too much to *take*. For the first time I had to stand in an unemployment line applying for $120 per week for living expenses. Mentally, it was a sudden death stroke to my ego and self-image. I had never felt so humiliated. My pride was shattered looking at the other individuals in the long line with me. Most gave the appearance of being uneducated, drug-addicted, vulgar individuals who were accustomed to living unproductively off the government. By language and attitude they seemed to have no intentions of working or becoming self sufficient. It was difficult to even raise my head to hold a conversation with any of them. Six months went by before I finally found a teaching position and was able to pull myself out of such a degrading situation.

Because of mismanagement, the club steadily headed toward disaster. Watching with my hands legally tied made me sick to my stomach. I wanted to disassociate myself from the corporation, but my repeated requests to Ray and Mo to buy me out were sarcastically ignored. I had initially borrowed money to purchase shares in the club but under present conditions did not have the means to pay back the loan. I would have been able to repay the loan if they only would have agreed to buy my interests. My financial struggles would have been over, because I would have invested the balance from my shares.

I expected my brother to be compassionate, understanding, and helpful when he saw me in my destitute state. But, no, he and his friend acted quite the opposite. Ray and Mo barely spoke to me, and when they did, it was short and caustic. They repeatedly told me that they had no obligation to me or interest to buy me out and there was nothing I could do about it. It was true as I only owned 23 percent of the stock. They were in the *driver's seat.*

Remembering our childhood together, when we shared one piece of bread among four siblings to survive, it seemed impossible that my brother could be so insensitive and cruel. Ray was my older brother and had been practically a father figure to me. He encouraged me when I was young and was always supportive of my educational, athletic, and career accomplishments. I could not believe that in our new country he had changed so much that he seemed purposely to want to destroy my life.

I thought about the many favors I had done both for him

and Mo and their families. Just procuring their permanent residency in America was reason enough for them to be indebted to me for the rest of their lives. Because of my timely help and support, they were among the few last lucky Iranians who were able to transfer their cash out of Iran without complications. The rate of exchange in 1976, when they moved, was 70 Rials to one U.S. dollar. The last I heard it was 1200 Rials to a dollar, with the government limiting $1,000 per person per exit visa.

While they were busy flying back and forth to Iran, tying up loose ends and securing good retirement salaries, I looked after their families. In their absence, I attended the PTA meetings for every child, was responsible for their schooling, medical assistance, grocery shopping, and did small home repairs. When I think back on it, I did the same things even when they were in America, as they seemed incapable of doing these simple tasks. Their rude and hurtful actions towards me was yet another excellent illustration of the troubles some Iranians create for themselves and their loved ones. Given the opportunity to benefit from a very sound investment, they threw it away. Instead, all our families suffered financially and emotionally, then and for years to come.

Their incompetence caused the membership at the athletic club to decline sharply and the business was spiraling toward bankruptcy. No one on the staff had the knowledge, genuine interest, or personal pride to make the business successful. Eight months after the Grand Opening, it was evident that minor repairs, maintenance, and direction were sorely needed. I could not bear to witness my pet project and a potentially sound business go under. So, with the advice of a reputable law firm, I made a final offer to Ray and Mo to sell their interest to me or buy my shares at the same price, rate, and conditions that I had offered them. Finally they admitted their inability to salvage the club and agreed to sell their interest to me.

During this same unhappy period, Hava took me to court several times. Her money-consuming court battles, without bearing fruitful results, created severe headaches, hardships, and additional financial losses for both of us. She, like some other "liberated" Moslem wives, made everyone's life more difficult by constantly taking the ex-husband to court.

To make matters worse, my brother on one of his frequent trips to Iran, brought my 67-year-old mother back with him and *dumped her on my lap*. Taking care of a person who truly was never a "mother" to me was an additional responsibility and burden along with all of my other worries at a time in which I had no solid job or income.

Even though I held no affection for my mother, I took care of her financially and physically for 42 years. In February 2000, she peacefully passed away at the age of 92. My mother abandoned us in Iran when we were small children. We later learned that she had married a Russian immigrant and had a son and a daughter with him. Her husband eventually took the children and returned to his homeland leaving my mother behind with no financial support. She had no place to live nor any means to survive. She came to me for help. I was 18 years old, living in a rented single room while I was a freshman in college.

The pressure on me from Hava's court fights and the loss of hope with the future of the athletic club became so much that for the first time in my life, I was tempted to commit suicide. I had no personal life, family, hope, interest, or ambition left in me. But being a true survivor, and remembering how my life had never been easy reminded me that I could find the determination to go on. All my life:

Whenever I was hungry, whenever I had pain,
I always could see the sunshine after the rain.
Many times I stumble, and often I fall
God has always been there,
To help me through it all!

In addition, I did not want to give Ray, Mo, and Hava the satisfaction of seeing me weak and falling apart. Also, the love for my daughters, wanting them to realize the dream I had for them to graduate from college, to be responsible citizens, and to enjoy the life and freedom of America.

It took me three months of dedicated, disciplined hard work to start digging myself and the club out of its abyss. Days started at 6 a.m. and barely finished by 11 p.m., seven days a week. First, I made the club financially self supportive and then turned it around to make it profitable. Five months later I found a buyer who purchased it for $1,100,000! Even though in my heart I did not want to sell, it was the only option. The other investors, who had put their trust in me, were thrilled with the outcome. They had previously lost all hope of recovering any of their invested money. Obviously, as the main stockholder after purchasing my brother's and Mo's shares, my percentage of the profit was substantial.

After I regained control of the club, rebuilt it, and sold it, Ray begged me to give him back all of the stocks that I had purchased from him. It was probably a silly expectation on his part as I remembered how he had treated me. But I wanted to prove I was a better human being and brother. I returned half of his shares to him, earning him a substantial profit. For my protection, I kept the other half, maintaining the majority control in the corporation. After the first go around, I no longer trusted him.

Taking the profit from his half of the shares, he then proceeded to file a lawsuit against me for two million dollars. He accused me of misrepresenting life in America and forcing him to leave Iran, which he said caused him great sadness and constant suffering. He fully expected the court to award him two million dollars! Fortunately for me, his lawsuit occurred in 1979, right during the heat of the American hostage crisis. The Boulder District Court judge, in his preliminary hearing, threw the case out stating that it was a waste of the court's time.

The ludicrous nature of Ray's court case reminded me of

the Saudi Arabian woman in Florida, who in May 2003 was suing the state because the Motor Vehicle Department would not allow her to leave her face covered, except for her eyes, for her license photo. Likewise, the judge threw her case out. The irony of the matter is how some immigrants quickly learn to take advantage of the legal system and freedom in America. Knowing that women are not allowed to drive in her old country, makes the matter rather hilarious, in a sad sort of way!

In 1981, Hava, the custodial parent, and now married to an American dentist and living in Greeley, Colorado threw our oldest daughter Sima out of their home. The divorce, lawsuits, and verbal battles between Hava and myself, plus Sima being a teenager, pushed our daughter into alcoholism and bad school performance. Her mother and step-dad, finding her to be too much to handle, wanted me to take the responsibility of taking care of her. Sima moved to Vail to live with me.

Sima was sixteen years old and cried the entire four-hour drive from Greeley to Vail. I comforted and assured her that I would do everything in my power to help her, if she would meet me halfway and was willing to cooperate. I told Sima it was up to her to make changes in her life, and if she did so, I would gladly support her one hundred percent. After so many years of separation, we both were very pleased to finally be together. We hugged in joy and commitment to each other. I was so happy to have my daughter with me and to be able to help her that I didn't even give a thought to changing the court decree with Hava, which proved to be a big mistake later.

On a more positive note, however, within two years Sima exhibited a 180 degree shift in her behavior. Not only did she not touch alcohol but she made the honor roll and graduated a semester early. She was a member of the relay team in high school track, winning the district championship. She excelled at tennis and could have received a scholarship to further her education or play professionally, but she was not interested in pursuing a tennis career. Sima was accepted at Colorado University in Boulder, which made me the proudest father on earth! She was accomplishing what every immigrant parent would hope for.

During her junior year at CU she met and became involved with a young man on campus. Sima's grades dropped because she placed more emphasis on doing her boyfriend's homework than her own. Hava and I shared her college expenses, one thing that we did agree upon. As educationally minded parents, both of us were more than happy to do this for our daughter. We wanted to provide Sima with the best opportunities for her future. Her decision to not pursue her education because of this less than noble young man was devastating. We were disappointed, and in our hearts and minds felt we could no longer support her financially because we both believed she was making a very bad choice.

Upset with us, Sima dropped out of college and on her own left for New York City. Years later she enrolled at New York University and earned her BA in Journalism. She is very talented, intelligent, and creative and we were hoping that with her skills and college education she would have chosen a better career and life than being a struggling actress in New York City and later in Los Angeles. Her choice has not pleased Hava nor me, but we accept it, as long as she is happy with her decision and lifestyle.

I wonder if Sima's independent nature was inherited from her mother or from my side of the family, as my mother was also a very unique individual. Even though my mother lived with me for many years, I never really understood her. She was among the first Iranian females who graduated from an American high school in Iran, under very dangerous conditions. Attending a non-Moslem school in the 1920's, opposing the wishes and influence of a majority of religious fanatics, was a risky thing to do. The police had to escort these girls to and from school each day to avoid possible harm by prejudiced citizens. If the Moslem fanatics had had their way, they would have stoned them to death. This occurred during the Shah Reza Khan's reign, father of the late Shah Reza Pahlavi, who had a very strong hold on the country and whom all the Moslem fundamentalists feared. Under the present Islamic government the existence of such a school would not be permitted. Because of her schooling, she was more of a Christian than a Moslem.

My mother, Rosa, exhibited little sense of humor and could not understand or even repeat a joke. It never occurred to her that people might be kidding at times. Her dry personality, plus her unfamiliarity with American expressions, created many occasions of entertainment for me.

Once when she was sick, I insisted on taking her to a doctor. Because she held on to certain traditional beliefs, Rosa had no desire to go, especially when she heard that the doctor was a male. Because of the serious nature of her illness, I had to practically *drag* her to the clinic. After a long wait in the examining room, which made my mother even more agitated, the doctor walked in humming to himself " do, do, do".....and then said: "What brought you here, Rosa?" She politely replied: "My son's car." He laughed, thinking that Rosa was joking with him. The doctor then asked, "I mean how can I help you, *young lady*?" She looked at him and said, "I am no young lady, I am old lady." The doctor unaware of her limited understanding of English, tried to cheer her up by saying: "*Oh no, come on, you are just a spring chicken*!" She got upset, picked up her handbag and said angrily: "I am no chicken, I am a nice old lady." Then she said to me in that special tone of voice, "Take me out of here; this man is crazy. I will not let him touch me!" I winked at the doctor giving him a little hint at what was happening. He immediately understood the predicament I was in and apologized to Rosa making her feel more comfortable and gave her a few free medications which made her even happier.

Another time, we were overnight guests in the home of a good friend of mine, whose name was Ted. In the early morning Ted was in the street in front of his house, flying a kite. Rosa, his wife and I were watching him from the window of the upstairs' guest bedroom. My mother *had a fit*, asking me why a mature man would be flying a kite? It's a children's past time. I said that he wanted to check the wind to decide what he was going to wear for the day. She gave me a funny look of distrust and disbelief.

Ted's several unsuccessful attempts prompted his wife to open the window to tell him what he was doing wrong. She yelled down, "Honey, *you need more tail*." Without a pause, Ted replied, "You better make up your mind, babe, because last night you told me to *go fly a kite*!" Rosa asked me to translate, but there was no way in the world I could tell her *what was going on*. So I told her, Ted said to his wife, "If you can do a better job, come on and take over."

In America the most difficult time I had with my mother was teaching her how to drive! Her lifelong dream of being able to sit behind the wheel and drive turned into a nightmare for me. But either because of my soft heart or stupidity, and against my better judgment, I taught her to drive, hoping to appease her in the latter years of her life. Afterward I felt sorry for all the other drivers on the road. Whenever she was driving, other cars had to get out of her way to be safe! Stop signs and stop lights, especially if they were on an incline, were touch-and-go for her. At times some individuals had to get out of their cars and push her car out of the way in order to be able to resume traffic. I was shocked beyond belief when she passed her driver's test!

A year after getting her license, she begged me every day if I would buy her a cheap, used car as it was her lifelong wish to own a vehicle! She kept repeating, "Wouldn't it be wonderful if I could write to all my friends and relatives in Iran that I now have my own car!" She promised me that she would never drive without me and stated that she just wanted to park the car in front of her apartment to *show off*, like the rich women in America. I could not convince her that, unlike the Middle East, there are ordinances and laws in this country which would not permit *junk* cars parked on the streets. But seeing her sad face each time, pleading with me, weakened me and I *caved in*. So, we visited a car dealership where she she chose a '75 Buick stick shift, which I thought she might not be able to handle. But she fell in love with it because its paint looked new and it was gigantic in size. It made my mother feel like she was in heaven! I wanted to buy her a small car with automatic transmission, which in my mind would have been easier for her to manage, but she fell in love with that over-sized green vehicle. She told me, "An automatic is not a car that mature people drive in Iran; it is for teenagers, not for me. What if my family comes and sees me driving a car like that? I would be embarrassed. This car has class!"

The car had a bumper sticker, which read, "*If you really love Jesus honk your horn.*" Because of her American schooling in Iran, she thought *it was cool*, and would not allow me to peel it off.

One day, she had a doctor's appointment but I could not get off work to take her. She insisted, "I can drive there by myself in my own car. I've practiced a few times, and I can drive around the block." When I asked her, "What about your promise to me that you would not drive without me," she convincingly answered, "What if you are not here, I have to take care of myself, don't I?" I did not think her driving to the doctor was a good idea. Besides her being a danger on the road, I was sure that she could not find her way in or out of the town. Therefore, I forced my young daughters to go with her. They were shocked that I would do such a thing to them, but I had no other choice.

At a very busy stop light, she was so excited and fascinated with her car and her driving that she did not notice the green light had changed twice. Meanwhile, all the drivers in the cars behind her were honking their horns and yelling and cussing at her. She could not believe what a "Jesus loving people" Americans were! My two girls scooted down in their seats as low as possible so that no one would recognize them, covering their faces behind their hands.

People were honking and screaming loudly, "Jesus Christ,

202

go; Jesus, go" and my innocent mother loved it, thinking it was all in support of her bumper sticker!

She told me, "It was just like your soccer match in the stadium, except they were cheering for me and my sticker. One man must have been from Hawaii, because he was leaning out his window and yelling *sunny beaches*. Another one was waving his hand at me, except with only one finger. He was screaming *"sunny beaches"* too. When I asked the girls why was he waving his hand like that, they giggled and told me, "Grandma, that is the Hawaiian good luck sign." Some people were so excited that they started to get out of their vehicles and walk toward us. By then, the light turned green and somehow I was the only one who made it through the intersection before the light turned red again. However, to show those nice people my appreciation, as I drove away, I waved and gave them all the Hawaiian good luck sign. Wasn't that nice?"

My daughters shook their heads and said, "That was the fourth time that the light had turned green, dad!" They begged me," Please, don't ever do that to us again. We were so scared and embarrassed that we didn't want anyone to see our faces."

The author with the late Florence Griffith Joyner,
an Olympic champion in 1984 and co-chair for the
Unites States Council in Physical Fitness and Sports.
November 1993

AFTER THE COLDEST NIGHT

In the mid-1980s I made an investment in a Video Production Company, a commitment which required much creativity and a challenge which I found to be fun. Producing well-presented, polished, professional videos for each and every project was extremely satisfying. Financially, however, it slowly became a disaster. I devoted five years of my life to it, but after suffering a $168,000 loss, I was forced to sell my beautiful home in Vail, unfortunately at a low, below-market price, to pay the debts to friends and investors. I felt morally compelled to repay those who had invested in my company because they believed in and trusted me. I still needed additional cash to pay the attorneys who had defended me in yet another unexpected lawsuit by Hava fourteen years after our divorce.

During the process of the lawsuit, needless to say I went back and forth to the bank in Vail. I spoke several times with a young woman employed there but had never been formally introduced to her. Her colleague Kim was my daughter Sima's best friend and an important witness in court against Hava's claim for unpaid child support.

One day while I was arranging Kim's transportation to court, I asked Kim to introduce me to Angelica. I thought that she was charming and chatting with her was about the only bright spot in my life. During our conversation, to my pleasant surprise I noticed that she was not wearing a typical wedding ring, which caught my attention as I always thought that she was married. Without giving it a second thought, I invited her to go out with me. She kindly thanked me for the invitation but apologized for not being able to accept because, in fact, she was married.

As it happened, about two months later Angelica was hoping to spend a day skiing with her husband. It was a Sunday but he was busy with his real estate sales and suggested that she call one of her friends. She tried but, because of other engagements, was unable to convince any of them to join her.

Disappointed, she started reading the daily newspaper and noted an article about Red Sandstone Elementary School having won the title of State Champion for the third time. The article included a picture of myself with some of my students.

Angelica looked up my phone number and thought that not only would she congratulate me but ask me if I would like to join her on that beautiful March day for some spring skiing. It was much too pretty of a day to be *cooped up* inside.

I had my documents for court all over the living room floor in preparation for Hava's latest absurd claim, which was about the most depressing way to spend a Sunday. The offer to go skiing instead, especially with cute Angelica, was irresistible; therefore, without letting her finish her sentence completely, I answered, "Love to."

We had a fabulous day together skiing. After the last run, I informed her that I was going to Boulder that night to stay with my girlfriend, because I had to deliver court papers to my attorney early the next morning. We parted saying what a great day we had together and that it would be fun to ski together again. Without seeing or talking with one another for the next week or so, the memories alone fueled some sort of chemistry which quickly began to explode beyond our control. Neither one of us expected this, and little did we realize that our lives would forever be entwined after only one day of skiing.

People, seeing our loving relationship, always want to know how we met and fell in love. With Angelica's permission, I share her story with you.

"Angelica's Story"

"Little did I know that in January 1990, when a dashing, blue-eyed foreigner walked into the bank where I was employed, that my life would be forever changed.

I was busy at my desk working when I looked up and he was standing there. When this handsome stranger spoke I was immediately intrigued. Where was he from? Who could he be?

206

Having traveled all over the world, I quickly tried to guess his accent, eliminating the ones with which I was familiar. Completely puzzled and curious, I unabashedly asked his place of birth. When he replied, "Iran," I was surprised. It had been years since I had known someone from Iran, which had occurred while living in Ankara, Turkey in 1961 and who was my very good friend, Farhad Sharif.

I must confess that I have always been fascinated by people from other countries. I think it's in my blood, as my mother is from Europe and my father is American. As an Air Force dependent, I spent much of my life overseas attending schools in Germany, Turkey, France, and Belgium and summers at my grandparents home in the Netherlands.

Parviz seemed so exotic, mysterious, and interesting to me. I must admit from the first meeting I was a bit smitten. That evening I called my mom, my best friend, and told her about Parviz Emamian. She laughed and said she knew of this blue-eyed Austrian. We both laughed when I told her that he was not Austrian but Iranian, and she acknowledged that made sense, as when she tried to strike up a casual conversation in German he never answered.

The next time he walked into the bank, for some strange reason my heart raced and I found it difficult to speak. I knew his name, although for the life of me I had a hard time saying it. With a twinkle in his eye, he teased me by saying he would never speak to me if I could not correctly pronounce his name.

I was 42 years old, married and acting like a teenager. I felt young, vulnerable, crazy, and foolish. I could not understand why this was happening to me, but I remember after that brief encounter hoping to catch a glimpse of him in a restaurant, on the street, or at a store. It was all so silly.

Weeks passed. It was Valentine's Day, a romantic American holiday. I was alone that evening because my husband was on a business trip out of town. He must have been quite busy as he had forgotten to call and my feelings were somewhat hurt. My fantasy stranger didn't call either, but of

207

course he didn't know that he should be calling, nor probably did he even remember my name.

Another month passed. It was March and a glorious time of year in the mountains. The weather was perfect with the sun shining, blue skies, and perfect snow. I wanted to go skiing but not alone. My husband again was busy and as I think about it, he never seemed to have enough time for me or to do things together.

Timidly, I decided to call Parviz, thinking what a wonderful day it would be if we could ski together, instead of my sitting at home. To my pleasant surprise he was at home and accepted.

Now that I thought that I had what I wanted, I was a total wreck. I must have changed ski suits five times, out of sheer nervousness and anticipation.

March 10th was the beginning of my present life, and all that I had known before was completely turned upside down. I was totally swept off my feet. Parviz was everything I had ever dreamed of - adventurous, sensitive, kind, caring, fun, good looking, plus a great ski instructor!

No, he didn't take me out for dinner with champagne and flowers that evening. Nor did our life together begin then. I went home, prepared dinner, and naturally was a complete mess. I was planning a St. Patrick's Day party, and I decided to add Parviz to our guest list. He declined at first, but with my persistence, and against his better judgment, he agreed.

At the party he was the center of attention, entertaining everyone, and teaching us how to belly dance. Everyone had such a good time!

I was uncontrollably drawn to him, like a magnet. A monumental decision, asking for a divorce, was made in a split second. My husband asked me to reconsider, offering to "pay off" Parviz to stay out of our lives. My husband said that we should get away, spend time with each other in Bermuda, and if that didn't work, he would send me to a psychiatrist. He kept asking how long I had known Parviz. When I told him that I had only skied with him one time, he truly believed I had lost my sanity.

Parviz and I were married on September 9, 1990, against the wishes of my family, friends, and former husband, all who thought I was out of my mind, marrying a "terrorist" and "wife beater." But, contrary to their beliefs, this day proved to be the most beautiful one of my life and I was the happiest woman in the world. I simply followed my heart.

I have learned so much from Parviz, because he is a teacher first and foremost. He can encourage, persuade, and push, not only a student but also me and probably anyone, beyond what he or she thinks possible to achieve. I have discovered that he is an astute businessman with a keen mind and he knows when to take a risk. I, on the other hand, except for matters of the heart, am very conservative. He's a wonderful husband, providing me with love, security, fabulous meals (he's an excellent cook!), and a lovely home. As a friend Parviz is always there, I couldn't ask for more. Now, my family and friends understand why I fell in love, and they too think the world of him."

Now, back to my narration........I was practically homeless, living temporarily as a caretaker in one room of the large house I had sold in Vail when I first met Angelica. Hava had my wages garnished for the amount of $14,300, which the judge awarded her at our last court hearing. In addition, because of the substantial loss I had from the video business, my ability to borrow from banks and lending institutions was *nil*.

Being without money, which has happened many times in my life, has never been a reason to consider myself poor. I believe that it is the way people think of themselves that gives them their image of self worth. I have always considered myself to be a very "rich" man, even without financial resources, because I have been blessed with good health, wonderful friends, and view myself as creative, educated, capable of earning a good living. Subsequently, I was able to sign a purchase contract on a repossessed town home in Avon,

Colorado for one third less than its actual value. I had fulfilled all the requirements for the purchase, except for $3,500 for closing costs. Even though I had no hope of obtaining a loan in any amount, giving up was not an option for me. Based on my persistent nature, I went to the bank to find out if a deal could be worked out.

As I walked in, I saw Angelica's pretty face, reminding me of the terrific day we had had together skiing, and almost making me forget why I had come to the bank. Unconsciously I walked straight toward her to start a conversation. After our friendly greeting, I explained my reason for being there, and asked her advice in pointing me to the loan officer who had the *biggest heart* at the bank.

I was stunned when she said to me, "You don't need to humble yourself by begging an officer for a loan. I know what you are going through, and it must be difficult enough. I have money in my savings account and would be more than happy to lend it to you." I was left speechless. While I did not want to accept her valuable offer, neither could I reject it.

Without waiting for my answer she handed me a check, which rather shocked me. Up to that moment, nothing but negative financial experiences had shaded my memories which involved female friends. The check that Angelica gave me actually saved me from destitution, and she didn't even ask for interest or a promissory note!

With the generosity, trust, and faith of Angelica, I was able to move forward and purchase the townhouse. Without telling her, I put her name on the deed. Six months later we were married and nine months after, with a little remodeling, we sold our first home together with a $65,000 profit! At last, I was out of debt with *money to spare.*

Upon retirement from teaching public school at the age of fifty seven, I was commended for my years of service with an accolade for "outstanding teacher" by the superintendent of Eagle County School District.

Angelica and I now live in Twin Lakes, which has to be one

of the world's most beautiful places. Surrounded by Colorado's highest mountains, it is "America's Little Switzerland."

Finding my wife Angelica, who truly is an angel, is a gift from heaven and Allah. With her love and sincerity, she has changed my bitter attitude toward marriage. Angelica became my bright guiding light during the darkest time of my life. Now, because of her I am a very happy man. She is my wife, lover, partner, and my best friend. Angelica is the reason I want to get up in the morning. I feel successful, content, and complete.

Four years ago, as I was reviewing my life while gazing at the lakes, the wildlife, the breathtaking scenery, and reflecting on my journey from Tehran to Twin Lakes, I felt compelled to share my story. I sincerely believe the success I enjoy at present is the direct result of the diligent efforts I made to immigrate to America in search of a better life. Because I am able to live in a free society, I have the privilege to publish this story. I can assure you that if I still lived in my former restrictive society, this book could never be in print.

Being a lifetime teacher, it has been difficult not to be surrounded by energetic students, striving to make a difference in someone's attaining his/her life-long goals. Therefore, after writing From Tehran to Twin Lakes, I accepted a position teaching geography at Colorado Mountain College in Leadville, Colorado. C.M.C. is the largest college in the state in regard to total student enrollment, having numerous campuses strategically placed in mountain towns and resorts to provide higher education for students who are also outdoor enthusiasts.

In the spring of 2001, I was offered the opportunity to be a Flagship Forum lecturer for Holland America Cruise Lines. What good fortune and *a feather in my cap!* And so, I retired once again. Lecturing on a cruise ship has been a wonderful way to meet interesting people from all over the world! I have found the passengers to be well-educated, astute, and informed. I learn from them as much as they gain new and different perspectives from me. To share my knowledge and life's journey is a most rewarding experience, and I have been encouraged to write more and better books because of the overwhelming and kind compliments I have received. Traveling with Holland America Lines and enjoying the quality of the service provided to their passengers and staff has been a memorable experience which I will cherish for the rest of my life.

I am forever grateful to Cheryl Fluehr for giving me the honor of being a part of the Holland America highly qualified staff, and I praise her for doing such a fantastic job of organizing unsurpassed shipboard entertainment and lecturers,

It is ironic that sometimes I compare my life to that of the late Shah of Iran, asking myself if, with all his wealth and power, did he have as much pleasure from life as I have had in my new country? I wonder how enjoyable or even painful his life was, knowing he could not go anywhere or do whatever he pleased without being surrounded by armed body guards protecting him from would-be assassins. How much stress and how little privacy must he have had under such circumstances!

At long last I am feeling at peace, and happy to take off the protective shield I have worn all my life. The poor, hungry, hopeless, homeless, and abused child has finally found a home!

Or so I idealistically thought! The tragic, heinous act of September 11, 2001, representing a strong message in opposition to the foreign policies of the United States in the Middle East and President Bush's subsequent response of initiating a war in Iraq has turned my world completely upside down. The sad attack, which was a total shock and unexpected disaster, in combination with the president's response of fighting terrorism by calling for a "crusade," has unfortunately opened a new chapter in my mind.

Frankly, the new Homeland Security Act created by our government, in addition to Mr. John Ascroft's changing of vital American laws, reminds me of living in Iran. It would appear now that our constitutional right of being innocent until proven guilty in the court of law has been taken away. I, or for that matter anyone, can be arrested and held for an unspecified time without a right to an attorney or family visitations. As I have stated previously, it is my strong personal belief that abject poverty and desperation in the Middle East are the main reasons for such turmoil and the suicide bombings in the region. Our government's war-like response, aggression, and legal restrictions will not resolve these problems.

Lamentably, I have reached the point where I do not feel safe nor happy in America knowing that we have made life more miserable for many poor, innocent people who had nothing to do with the politics or wrong doings of dictators. In addition, it is my conviction that our President, along with John Ascroft, has created a "nation of fear." Because of these convictions, and having written my book Islam versus Terrorism, I am uncertain if I would like to live my few good remaining years under such progressively, undesirable conditions.

I am strongly persuaded to believe that President Bush, supported and encouraged by his war hungry, capitalistic associates and cabinet members, lied to us by linking Saddam Hussein to the Al-Qaeda, the ones responsible for 9/11 and by misrepresenting the threat of Saddam's supposed weapons of mass destruction. He has America embroiled in a double war that will more than likely go on for years and will in the process take the lives of many innocent American soldiers, as well as Afghanis and Iraqis.

Furthermore, the reported inhumane treatment of the "detainees" in Quantanamo Bay for the past two years, in blatant disregard of the Geneva Convention, is a shameful reflection of the deterioration of American ideals and principles. If, after such a long period, these prisoners have not given any information, they either don't know anything or realistically we would not be able to obtain anything more without severe torture and death. These events and conditions for the first time have made me feel NOT so proud of my country nor of being an American citizen.

I only hope that at this stage of my life I will have enough years left to be able to adapt, adjust, and assimilate to another new country, New Zealand. My wife and I wish not to live in constant turmoil and fear. We are preparing and willing to make one more monumental change in our lifestyles in hopes of living in peace. We have chosen the city of Nelson, located on the South Island overlooking the Tasman Bay as our new home.

The beauty of the South Island is found in its open spaces, its sheep and deer farms, vineyards, orchards, pine plantations, palm trees, lakes, water falls, mountains, sand dunes, and beautiful sunny beaches. Nelson is consistently the sunniest city in New Zealand and attracts people from around the world to enjoy its international restaurants, sidewalk cafes, parks, shops, and fresh vegetable and fruit markets. There's a Mediterranean air about this whole area and its surrounding seaside villages. Nearby Abel Tasman National Park is an outdoor lovers' paradise, an extensive park which protects a beautiful stretch of coastline with hiking trails, camping spots, water taxis, sailboats and kayaking.

I have found the people of New Zealand to be extremely open-minded, honest, generous, friendly, helpful, with a wonderful wit and sense of humor. The only concern I have is learning English the New Zealand way! I am finally *getting the hang* of American English and I hope that learning the New Zealand English is not going to be much of problem at this stage of my life!

Having to learn a new language now reminds me of another cute joke. The European Union Commissioners have announced that agreement has been reached to adopt English as the preferred language for European communications, rather than German, which was the other possibility.

As part of the negotiations, her Majesty's government conceded that English spelling had some room for improvement and has accepted a 5 year phase-in plan for what would be known as Euro-English.

In the first year, "S" will be used instead of the soft "C." Sertainly, this will make sivil servants jump with joy. The hard

"C" will be dropped in favor of the "K." Not only this should klear up konfusion, but keyboards kan have one less letter.

There will be growing publik enthusiasm in the sekond year, when the troublesome "PH" will be replaced by "F." This will make words like "fotograf" 20 per sent shorter.

In the third year, publik akseptanse of the new spelling kan be expekted to reach the stage where more komplikated changes are possible. Governments will enkorage the removal of double letters, which have always been a deterent to akurate speling. Also, al wil agre that the horible mes of silent "E"s in the languag is disgrasful, and should go away.

By the fourth year, people wil be reseptiv to steps such as replasing "TH" with "Z" and "W" with " V."

During ze fifz year, ze unesesary "O" kan be dropd from vords kontaining "OU," and similar changes vud of kors be aplid to ozer kombinations of letas.

Und after ze fifz yer, ve vil have a rali sensible riten styl. Zer vil be no mor truble or difikultis and evervun vil find it ezi to spik German like zey vunted in ze forst plas. Ze drem of an united urop vil finali kum tru!

Considering all the obstacles that one must overcome, I strongly feel that with proper planning, enough time, a lofty spirit and an honest approach and attitude, every immigrant can have the healthiest root, producing the best fruits to harvest for the rest of their lives, just as I am now tasting. It took a long time, was not easy or the fairy tale I thought it would be, but I have enjoyed the freedom which every individual in the world should be entitled to.

I wish the very best to all the immigrants throughout the world. It is my desire to let people know, whether they are immigrants or not, that they too can have it all if they "go for the gold." Thinking positive and putting the past behind is the key to success. We must all remind ourselves that to make a significant difference in our personal lives and in society there is only one way to go, and that is forward! "This is it."

I wish that somehow my grandmother Tala could know that, after the darkest, coldest night, I am now living in a bright new day.

Grandmother Tala with my two sisters and me
Tehran - 1948